CHRISTIANS *and* CHURCHES
of AFRICA

Books Published
by Orbis Books
in the
Theology in Africa Series

In keeping with its mission to publish works by authors from the Third World (or "Global South") Orbis Books collaborates with Regnum Africa in Ghana and Editions Clé in Cameroun to bring outstanding works on African theology and religious reflection from both Francophone and Anglophone Africa. These books are part of these two publishers' "Theological Reflections from the South" Series, which may in time include books from Asia and Latin America.

Other books published in the Series

Kwame Bediako, *Jesus and the Gospel in Africa: History and Experience*

Mercy Amba Oduyoye: *Beads and Strands: Reflections of an African Woman on Christianity in Africa*

Theology in Africa Series

CHRISTIANS
and
CHURCHES
of AFRICA

SALVATION IN CHRIST
AND BUILDING A NEW AFRICAN SOCIETY

Kä Mana

ORBIS BOOKS
Maryknoll, New York 10545

Founded in 1970, Orbis Books endeavors to publish works that enlighten the mind, nourish the spirit, and challenge the conscience. The publishing arm of the Maryknoll Fathers and Brothers, Orbis seeks to explore the global dimensions of the Christian faith and mission, to invite dialogue with diverse cultures and religious traditions, and to serve the cause of reconciliation and peace. The books published reflect the opinions of their authors and are not meant to represent the official position of the Maryknoll Society. To obtain more information about Maryknoll and Orbis Books, please visit our website at www.maryknoll.org.

The original French title of this book is *Chrétiens et églises d'Afrique penser l'avenir.* It was first published in English as *Christians and Churches of Africa Envisioning the Future: Salvation in Christ and the Building of a New African* Society in 2002 in the "Theological Reflections from the South" Series by Editions Clé (B.P. 1501, Yaoundé, Cameroun) and Regnum Africa (P. O. Box 76, Akrpong-Akuapem, Ghana), as part of Regnum Books International (P.O. Box 70 Oxford OX2 6HB, United Kingdom) for the International Fellowship of Evangelical Mission Theologians, formed of the African Theological Fellowship, the Latin American Theological Fraternity (José Marmol 1734, 1602 Florida, Buenos Aires, Argentina), and Partnership in Mission Asia (P. B. 21, Vasant Vihar, New Delhi 110 057, India)

Manufactured in the United States of America.

Library of Congress Cataloging in Publication Data

Kä Mana.
    [Christians and churches of Africa envisioning the future]
    Christians and churches of Africa : salvation in Christ and building a new African
      society
    / Kä Mana.
      p. cm.
    Includes bibliographical references.
    ISBN 1-57075-544-2 (pbk.)
      1. Christianity--Africa. 2. Christian sociology--Africa. I. Title.

BR1360.K23 2004
276'.083--dc22

                                         2004049552

Contents

PREFACE

This book is the second to be issued in English in the series, 'Theo-logical Reflections from the South', a new initiative of the Centre de Littérature Évangélique - Editions Clé, in association with Regnum Africa, devoted to the promotion of Christian literature in two of Africa's *linguae francae*, English and French. The title has already appeared in French, *Chrétiens et églises d'Afrique penser l'avenir*.

The aim of the series 'Theological Reflections from the South' is to publish and jointly disseminate with other African publishers, including Haho Publishers (Lomé, Togo) and Regnum Africa (Akro-pong, Ghana) selections of existing writings, or new texts, by eminent theologians from the South, that is, from Africa, Central and South America and Asia.

At the time when the centre of gravity of the Christian world has shifted from the West to the Two-Thirds World, it seems particularly important for us to promote theological writings emerging from the South and make them available across linguistic barriers.

The launching of this series was facilitated by the Reverend Ype Schaaf, founder of Editions Clé. The series enjoys the support of the Africa Desk of the Uniting Churches of the Netherlands and other church and Christian agencies.

This English edition has been produced by Regnum Africa, the publishing arm of the African Theological Fellowship.

The Publishers

CHAPTER 1

Introduction

Salvation as the orientation of life:
A search for the right interpretation

Whatever the variety of forms it has taken in societies, and the powerful rhythms it has inculcated in its innumerable modulations through centuries, the problem of salvation has always been for mankind, a problem of an essential spiritual quest for the meaning of existence, and the fundamental search for the ultimate orientation of life.

In its multifaceted forms, this problem involves simultaneously:

- the quest for origins and foundations from which meanings emerge, meanings which allow mankind or a community to understand and organise itself in the heart of history;

- the formulation and establishment of the principles of unity capable of ensuring a coherence of being to a society as a whole and the groups which comprise it; of endowing them with a web of common images, representations and values deeply experienced and accepted as indisputable canons for guiding existence, structuring life and taking action;

- the development of a clear vision of goals by a community in relation to its future, its relationship with transcendence and its aspiration towards the world beyond.[1]

If we consider these three dimensions of meaning as a framework in which we can understand, reflect upon and present the African perception of Jesus Christ and the problem of salvation, we must ask ourselves the following questions:

- What are the African worlds of meaning and the dynamics of local interpretations which constitute the basis of christological quests in theological research and of the human preoccupations in which Christ is called upon as a person and as the gospel?

- According to what images and systems of value does Africa's understanding of Jesus Christ as a reality, as a social dynamic and as a promise of salvation, function today?

- As a society, where exactly are we heading with regard to the gospel? What ideals do we carry, and what chance do we have of fulfiling them in our ultimate quests for transcendence, and in our vision of the world beyond?

A fundamental problem for future challenges

The questions raised here may seem abstract and without any bearing on the most crucial problems such as the abject poverty and grinding misery which our societies are confronted with each day, and which leave them without any glimmer of hope:

- moral helplessness in confronting illness, deep distress in the face of supernatural forces, and the irrepressible need for healing and deliverance from the forces of darkness;

- the powerlessness of our societies in the face of the 'geopolitics of chaos'[2] which make up our world today, and the disconcerting policies imposed by international financial institutions;

- the implosion of our creative forces in the unspeakable anarchy experienced by many of our countries where the quest for survival generates violence and an instinct that is destructive of life itself;

- the multiplication of hotbeds of social unrest and areas of armed conflicts in a continent where the basic needs of life are far from satisfactory, and where the countries with the most appaling cases of poverty in the world are found.

Today, it is impossible not to see clearly the urgency of these problems and how they relate to the dynamics of hope by which many Africans refuse to give way to the logic of despair, as they forge for themselves a destiny that is in keeping with their dreams. Through political action, socio-economic commitment, cultural research and spiritual quests freed from the debilitating tendency to apathy, these Africans once again want to realise their vision for the continent, and build together a destiny of happiness, dignity, justice, freedom and responsibility.

If one realises that this arena, full of despair and at the same time also full of a vigorous will to hope, is the vital space from which christological quests develop as a search for salvation in Africa, then the needed reflection consists in clearly showing in what way Jesus of Nazareth is a catalyst for changing life, a lever for raising the future, a ferment for bringing in a new society and a solution to the ultimate questions about death and the world beyond.

What is important is to re-examine African quests for salvation, that is, the meaning of existence and of life, from the perspective of the fight against the forces of evil and decay, and of darkness and death. In all these realities, the person, message and ideals of Jesus Christ undoubtedly represent a universal solution to our African crisis: the seed of a new passion for living and of a new spirit of resourcefulness for building our future.

Areas of research and engagement

The focus of our study in the light of these demands, will include identifying the areas of African quests for salvation and meaning, from which a christology for overcoming the crisis, for social transformation, and for the building of a new society can be established and take root in our spirits, our consciences and our creative imagination.

In accordance with the three-fold understanding of salvation as basis, unity, and goal, it should be said that as Africans, we view salvation in Jesus Christ from the following perspectives:

- we view it especially from the primordial place where our ancestors of old handed down to us great wisdom, tools of knowledge, customs and lifestyle, through which we may welcome Jesus Christ as one of us, deep within the 'grove of initiation',[3] in this ancestral hearth, vital energy which determines our identity as a people, civilisation and culture;

- we also view it from our current socio-cultural and politico-economic challenges and the global crisis, against which we have been struggling from the dawn of modern times till today. This is a serious and multidimensional crisis which constitutes the main problem of our destiny today, and a real test for our minds and imagination;

- finally, we view Jesus Christ against the background of all our religious ideals and spiritual powers where Christianity occupies an equally important place alongside Islam and African traditional religions.[4]

From this three-fold point of departure, there emerge orientations of christological research within which three main fields may be identified:

The first area of research and study concerns the fundamentals of our existence and life in Africa, and the basis of our culture and vision of the world. The problem Africa faces in this quest for salvation, is how insignificant we seem to be in today's world, how great are the shortcomings that hinder us, and the extent to which we debase ourselves in our own eyes as individuals, as a culture and as a society.

What should be done today in order for us to become people

with meaning for our lives as individuals and as a society? It is time
to reconnect with the most cardinal forces of our culture and of our
lives. For it is on the basis of this answer that a meaningful christology as the basis or foundation of the quest for salvation, can develop
today.

The second area is that of vital mechanisms which we employ in
order to fight against both our socio-economic and political situation
and our dire material straits; against our moral decay, our existential despair and our spiritual collapse in the face of the supernatural
forces that oppress us, and which make our societies cry out fervently
to God for deliverance and healing.

What vision do we have of our salvation here and now? How do
we respond in order to be able to change our societies and overcome
the crisis which stifles our creativity? What strategies for change can
we adopt in overcoming the difficulties of life?

By looking at the efforts made by Africans to overcome their societal crisis, we can attempt to develop a coherent christology as a
force for transforming social norms, by applying principles and
values capable of quickening our conscience and enriching the imagination of society today.

- The third area of our quest for salvation in Africa, is our perception of the future: the wellspring of our ideals and the building up of
a new society. Men and women everywhere in Africa are looking
ahead to the future and seek to move creatively in the direction of a
cultural rebirth, economic, political and spiritual revival, as a basis
for the new society in our countries.

What does this quest for salvation contribute to christological
thought today? How can the personality of Jesus Christ be made an
integral part of this search, and also be made the basis of a new
destiny and force behind a new universal meaning to our existence?
These questions open up the prospect of a new christology as foundational in building a new African society.

The focus of our study

In this study, we hope to bring out the African quests for salvation
which are centred around Jesus of Nazareth, and to reinforce the
African's perception of Christ whereby in our search for meaning in
life, we find in the Messiah of Galilee a rich source for renewing our
being and destiny.

We will consider this problem from two angles. On the one hand,
the connection between Christ as the way to salvation and the source
of inspiration of the indigenous myths of African society and

culture, and, on the other hand, the spiritual authority of the message of Jesus Christ and the present situation of Africa as it faces the future.

In the next eight chapters, we shall reflect on the figure and personality of Jesus Christ, based on current research in the historical origins of African culture, and on the vital principles which have influenced the African's world view from time immemorial.

By considering the way African Egyptologists and custodians of our cultural traditions view the problem of our human and societal crises, we can understand Jesus Christ in a new way and become aware of the perspectives on salvation which he freely offers us in the decisive dialogue which it is helpful to establish with him in the heart of the 'grove of initiation',[5] which give our destiny its fundamental principles and its essential values.

Beginning from the Egyptology research of Cheikh Anta Diop and Théophile Obenga, and passing through Hampâté Ba's study of African traditions to the works of theologians such as John Mbiti and Oscar Bimwenyi-Kweshi, a research field has developed where a number of young researchers seek to find the meaning of our destiny as culture and as civilisation.

Because of our own involvement in this in-depth research and our own concern to include African theological thought in African history as a whole, we make the effort to give due weight to the findings of this research.

In the last three chapters of our study, we place ourselves in the perspective of present-day Africa, and view its socio-cultural and politico-economic problems as a framework within which the question of salvation in Jesus Christ is considered.

Convinced that the challenge today is to re-define our destiny in the world, we intend to integrate the spirit of Africa's founding myths and that of the Christian faith into a new spiritual understanding of our present history. We shall do this by combining the theoretical and practical aspects, as is already being done by African Christians, through extensive research and practical activity for the sake of the salvation of the continent.

Footnotes

[1] Cf. Zaki Laïdi, *Un monde privé de sens* (Paris: Fayard, 1994).

[2] This is the title of a very useful book by Ignacio Ramonet on the reality and management of power in the world, after the collapse of the Soviet empire and the opening of the Pandora's box of globalisation under the leadership of the

United States of America (Paris, Editions Galilée, 1997). In the light of Ramonet's analysis, we think it is not certain that the economic and financial policies based on the interests of major international trusts and guaranteed by the IMF and the World Bank constitute the way to salvation for people facing woes of underdevelopment. Instead of being an 'Order' which promotes life, these policies constitute a factor of serious disorder from which nothing really human can be obtained. What is important for the people who are suffering a great deal, is to oppose the new powers that are dominating the world today, and to open new ways for the future. This is an urgent task for the African continent where it is still wrongly believed that structural adjustment policies will help us overcome the crisis and will also enable us to develop a new society. The time has come for a new proposal and for credible alternatives.

3 Here I quote Oscar Bimwenyi-Kweshi, a Congolese theologian who has made this expression the basis of any pertinent African theological discourse today. His book, *Discours théologique africain, problèmes des fondements* (Paris: Présence Africaine, 1981) remains so far the major reference text on the questions of encounter between Christ and Africa.

4 Reference may be made here to my book: *Christ d'Afrique: les enjeux éthiques de la foi africaine en Jésus Christ* (Paris: Karthala, 1994). My reflections here follow on from this book in a perspective which professional theologians describe as soteriological, i.e., of salvation and its requirements for the life of mankind.

5 French: bosquet initiatique. This is a figurative expression to describe the symbolic source of the collective cultural memory and historical consciousness of African peoples.

CHAPTER 2

Field of research and problems encountered

Our reflection here is drawn from two areas of research with which we are now involved. It gives an account of ground-swells of thought which shape the project and the methodology by which we approach the question of salvation in Jesus Christ.

Two research initiatives

There is first, the Academy of African Thought which conducts research on the origins of black culture. It is a learned society that operates on the model of institutions in the sociological sense described by Michel Crozier, as 'not clear structures but rather groups of persons, adequately varied, at the risk of being somewhat diffuse; groups in which there are co-operative relationships directed towards the acquisition of an effective way of reasoning rather than techniques and methods'.[1]

Led by Congolese Egyptologist, Guillaume Bilolo Mubabinge, and a group of African researchers from various academic disciplines who got together to run a publishing house, 'Publications Universitaires Africaines' (Kinshasa-Libreville-Munich), the Academy has, as its central guiding principle of approach and reasoning:

- the centrality of Africa as an initiating force in the analysis of problems, in the clarification of what is at stake, and in the quest for the most appropriate solutions to given data;
- 'the absorbing opening'[2] through which one integrates within oneself the great dynamics of the human which the vast world of civilisations and cultures offers Africa;
- the reciprocal critique between what springs from the heart of our African culture, and what comes to us from other cultures;
- the common invention of the future through the assumption of responsibility for the ideals by which people can together build the future of humanity.

These principles mean that Africa, viewed from the perspective of its total history, must have had myths of origins, sought solutions to its essential problems, defined ways of living and surviving, imagined ways of being creative, and developed lifestyles full of potential for future generations.

Thus, Africa constitutes not only a rich repository of available knowledge and wisdom, but also a place for welcoming modes of reasoning, creative ideals and critical questions from other areas. These must be perceived and received as seed in good soil, with the prospect of building a new society at the very heart of thought and action peculiar to African societies.

The second initiative is the SCAT Academy for Research in Egyptology and African culture. It consists of a group of about twenty researchers led by Professor Fabien Kange Ewane of the University of Yaoundé (Cameroon).

The aim here is to take up once again the creative cultural abilities of ancient Africa and those of traditional societies, in order to integrate them into the world of today or more precisely, to re-discover the ancestors and their legacy as a starting point for planning the future. Ancestors, here refer to the energy and fresh initiative with which 'the Fathers and Mothers' of African culture developed a vision of the world and organised a space for living which they bequeathed to us as an inalienable legacy.

What we seek to do, is to develop a tradition of thought which helps to encourage every African man and woman to develop a moral sense of their social responsibility, a conscience enriched by the faith which Africa has in itself, its history, its destiny and in its ability to promote credible alternatives to political, economic, social and cultural crises of the contemporary world order.

A crucial problem which affects all Africans

There is one problem that is common to all researchers in these two learned societies within which we have undertaken our theological, philosophical, political and spiritual research; and that is: what is the situation of the African in today's world, and what are his real prospects for living in the future?

In spite of the diversity of our intellectual journeys, the multiplicity of our fields of research and the variety of our questions, as researchers, we have all been struck by the inability of contemporary African societies to resolve the fundamental problems confronting them.

In the many discussions we have had during our working sessions, conferences, colloquia, seminars, symposia, workshops and study groups, we have never stopped asking ourselves why this should be so, a question which, in fact, relates to the true state of our cultures, societies and their creative capacities.

'Why, as Africans, can we not respond adequately to the challenges of our destiny? Why are we paralysed when confronted with problems that only we can resolve? What is wrong with our mental and intellectual capabilities to make us give way to the forces of defeatism so easily, and in such a disturbing manner?'

Because most of us studied in major, distinguished European and American universities, we know that our intellectual and theoretical capabilities in research are equal to those of our colleagues overseas. We also know that given similar or equal conditions of work, we are capable of facing up to the major scientific challenges of our era, and to what the future may hold, with optimism and serenity.

Why then can we not produce effective weapons for the struggles of today? Why can we not create conditions for a destiny worthy of our true possibilities, organise ourselves according to the objectives of dignity and prosperity, and contribute in a decisive manner to the emergence of a new civilisation which would be beneficial to all of humankind?

Similarly, research sessions which we carried out among our people and in different sectors of society in the remotest of our rural areas, reveal a wealth of rich ideas, vision, creativity, potential and inventive dynamism, which can serve as foundations for the future.

Why have these treasures remained silent, hidden, and unused at a time when we need them most in all areas of our lives? Why does the moral, spiritual, medical, scientific, political, economic and social legacy of Africa not help us to face up to the challenges of the future?

Confronted with these questions, we realised that the main problem is not our intellectual capacity nor the knowledge we acquired in the course of our training; and lies even less in the quality of intellectual achievements and vital knowledge which constitute our cultural legacy. The problem is rather that of our present existence and actions, and our own perceptions of our culture and civilisation in the current context, where, in the words of Achille Mbembe, 'the challenge is to create another picture of ourselves in the world'.[3]

More precisely, our problem is that of the lack of significance that tends to characterise our existence; the inconsistencies and loss of a proper sense of our self-worth which show up in all areas of our lives.

In order to get to the root of this issue, and to reflect upon it essentially as the question of what meaning to confer on African existence at the dawn of the third millennium, we have decided to examine it from two points of view.

The first concerns the global impression we give of ourselves to the world, and the second concerns the underlying structures which determine our actions and our very existence today.

Striking images and impressions of a continent in crisis

What is implied at this initial stage? It concerns a global patholog-ical impression we give of ourselves and which can be defined as follows:
- lack of an inner centre of gravity from which to derive our sense of value in building the future of humankind;
- absence of a principle of social organisation for the entire conti-nent, an organisation which can bring about concrete, ambitious and feasible projects in all major areas that are crucial to the development of human societies today;
- a serious underestimation of our own capabilities and of our historical ingenuities, 'the negative image' we have of ourselves, as Achille Mbembe puts it.

The notion of insignificance

Let us first consider this feeling of our own insignificance that we have experienced since independence. In the quest for political philos-ophy, contemporary social anthropology and analysis of current African literary production, this problem is revealed to us through works from which we drew a number of conclusions.[4]

At the dawn of independence and also during the period charac-terised by military dictatorships, we saw Africa undergo a crisis as a result of truly insignificant people who usurped power and occupied leadership positions in many of our African states, as the guides of our destiny. Apart from a few who left behind fond memories of their reign, many of our Heads of State did not have what it takes to build for the future.

These leaders were totally ineffective, mentally bankrupt and lacked any political will, deficiencies camouflaged by pompous and verbose speeches. They resembled puppets who repeated formulae prepared elsewhere, and implemented measures planned in other countries. They appeared shallow and lacked the strength of character needed to enable them to lead the people.

Their insignificance is expressed in the following characteristics which were brought to light through our research on the novels of A. Fantouré, A. Kourouma and P. Ngandu-Nkashama.[5]

Their innate shallowness

Despite the pseudo-revolutionary rantings, deceptive ideological theories, their formidable security apparatus and constant dealing with supernatural forces, nothing in them spoke of strong convictions serving a great cause. Lacking the confidence of having a basic plan capable of mobilising an entire people, they could not instil in the people the only motivation that gives value to a person: the embodiment of all the dreams of a community. They had no values other than their own private interests, and their position as servants of unscrupulous masters or partners. They had the semblance of power, but had lost touch with real power, which is the ability to build a great destiny together with the people they ruled.

Since the people had no faith in them, they could not rely on their creative force and resourcefulness. These 'leaders' therefore indulged themselves in idle talk, ideological ramblings and in political delusions.

After their game of contrivance, for which the people paid a heavy price in suffering and loss of life, they disappeared in a pitiful manner, rejected by their people, betrayed by their masters and partners and condemned to admit at the end of their life, what they really were - worthless people.

Their appaling triviality

This means that they never gave serious consideration to themselves as human beings, and to their destiny. Their lives were a pretence and they manipulated the semblance of power to conceal their lack of real authority. They never thought of engaging in a profound introspection that would cause them to think about the meaning of their mission and the gravity of their responsibilities in the light of history. They did not examine problems with all the seriousness they deserved, but rather took decisions on an ad hoc basis, often listening to the last speaker and riding roughshod over the real concerns of their people, investing in flashy and ridiculous things.

They lacked personality and could not understand the real issues of the situation they were supposed to manage. They trusted in pseudo-experts, so-called specialists, fortune tellers, and officially recognised praise singers. They thus distanced themselves from the people, and resorted to terror and violence to maintain their grip on power.

Consequently, they became little bandits at the head of incredible wealth which they deposited or invested abroad. They believed it was safe there, until political setbacks made them realise that their sense of security was a mere illusion, deriving from ignorance of human destiny and the vanity of power.

Their inner emptiness

No one could say by merely looking at them whether the ideas they put together to form some 'crazy' ideology arose from any human strength which they could rely on. The impression they gave was that of thoughtless beings, without any major reasoning ability, without human imagination, and without concern for a job 'well done' except for dishonourable tasks like torture, assassinations and embezzlement of funds meant for the development of their people.

Although, like empty vessels, they made a lot of noise, they fooled nobody, not even their aides, nor their people, nor even themselves. Even if they were able to surround themselves with all the spiritual-ists, diviners, marabouts and religious leaders of the world, that would not in any way confer any spirituality on them; nor would call-ing upon the best brains in their pseudo-empires add to their wisdom in any way. One only has to refer to the genius of popular inventive-ness to see what the masses think of them and how cartoonists see them: totally empty beings, devoid of humanity.

Their senseless logic

This means that their whole life was dominated by the lack of a right perception and understanding of the essential issues in life. Like the fool in the Bible who says 'God does not exist', they thought they were masters of visible and invisible mysteries, and mistook them-selves for God, forgetting that they were ordinary mortals; and like yet another 'fool' who piled up riches upon riches until he was told by the Master of Destiny: 'Madman, this very night, your soul will be taken from you', these charlatan leaders planned their destiny *per omnia saecula saeculorum*, thinking that the circus or operetta that they called power, would be eternal. Lacking the right perception of reality, they abandoned their responsibility and took refuge in the shadow of their insignificance.

Their fundamental absurdity

The entire system of power which they set up leads nowhere. It has neither a human goal nor a vision of hope. The only legacy they leave upon their death, is the sound of their hollow speeches and the dreadful nightmare the people experienced under their reign. It is only then that the people are able to assess the incredible evil power and the unfathomable depth of darkness under which they have lived.

Their human mediocrity

There is a sharp contrast between the qualities of excellence, will power and commitment required by their heavy responsibilities, and the lack of seriousness they exhibit in the discharge of their daily duties. The excellence of their office is matched, in fact, only by their mediocrity, the lack of any concern to live up to what is expected of them, and to prove to their people that they possess the ethical fortitude that could make them leaders of people.

Their hopeless duplicity

From our experience of them, we knew very well that they were unreliable, charlatans, and very far from all that the word truth stands for in meaning and with respect to human values. The promises, which they love to repeat among themselves, some of which are quotes from their masters, their electoral speeches or other, in fact, appeal only to those who are naive enough to believe them. In their sham, false, make-believe empire, their relationship with their people is that of unscrupulous charmers, inhuman, cold and calculating manipulators.

The characteristics that contribute to the emptiness of our politicians have long been at the heart of the discussions of our researchers. In trying to understand the basic mechanisms by which our societies function, we have come to the same conclusion as the Cameroonian philosopher, Fabien Eboussi Boulaga, that, 'people have the leaders they deserve'.

At first, that conclusion seemed rather extreme to us, unfair and even false. It was not possible to believe that the policies implemented by Sékou Touré, Ahmadou Ahidjo, Joseph-Désiré Mobutu Sese Seko, Idi Amin Dada, Jean-Bédel Bokassa, Macias Nguéma and many others like them today, could be interpreted as complicity between the people and their leader, as was said in the times of Zairean authenticity, between 1970 and 1980.

The way all these 'leaders' have ended their reign, by being disowned, or rejected by their people, prevented us from drawing conclusions about the support given them by their people for policies they imposed on their countries. And yet, looking at it more closely, we have become conscious, as African intellectuals, of the determining factor of a sense of worthlessness in our own being and in our own quests.

In determining the major responsibility of African policy-makers in the planning and strengthening of military dictatorships and bloody regimes, we have been led to analyse the evil from which Africa suffers, from the point of view of the thoughtlessness, futility, 'madness', mediocrity, deceitfulness, and absurdity of Africa's intellectual elite.

One cannot deny today the role played by some educated people, such as Edem Kodjo, in providing the intellectual undergirding for the one-party state in Togo, Gambembo Mfumu wa Untadi, the philosopher, in the strengthening of Mobutu's ideology in Zaïre, or Professor Augustin Kontchou Kouomegni for his intellectual support to Cameroon's 'New Deal' policy.

We have seen clearly that the combination of unworthy politicians and an unworthy intellectual class, imposed on our societies the unproductive reasoning that prevailed during the years of single party rule.

Even in the present quests for democracy as our 'new independence', to quote Eboussi Boulaga again, intellectuals continue to be blind supporters of those who are at the helm of the State. They provide them with concepts, theories and deceptive ideologies that conceal their total refusal to submit to the will of the people through free, fair and transparent elections.

No wonder people 'trained' by insignificant leaders and 'enlightened' by insignificant intellectuals, have themselves sunk into insignificance. In the end, they have internalised rules of life that lead to death and exuded adulation of corrupt power, without asking questions about this very drift to moral and political catastrophe.

One cannot understand the 'madness' of the Zaïrean people under Mobutu's regime, the ethnic.cleansing of the nation under Juvénal Habyarimana in Rwanda, the pervasiveness of criminal activities in Nigerian society under the rule of the generals, as well as the apathy of the people of Central Africa under Bokassa's tragi-comic empire, if one does not take into account this hypothesis of an osmosis between the mind of the leader and that of the people, in the disintegration and ultimate destruction of the society. It is this very disintegration and destruction that take the form of insignificance, that makes everyone lose the sense of direction for the future.

An examination of the dreams of the masses, the recurrent messages of the music that 'sells well' and the many tunes to which all are forced to dance, could only comfort us in the notion of placing the concept of insignificance at the centre of our philosophical analysis of the African situation. Rarely do popular dances, music, and dreams lead us to our inner selves without seeking to distract us and make us delirious, like dangerously sick and mad black people.

The problem of inconsistency

Let us now consider the problem of inconsistency in our actions. We realise that the concept of the worthlessness of our being is closely linked to the inconsistency of our actions.

Whilst our worthlessness places us before the massive fact of a cast of mind that is unaware of the depth of being and succumbs to the dictatorship of the nameless and the tyranny of futility, the inconsistency of action shows the difference between problems as they are and the social intelligence mobilised to solve them. In our countries, this difference has become a real chasm, and our social intelligence so off-target with regard to the impulses that lead to action.

Many researchers have pondered over the 'crisis of African intelligence' in order to determine its magnitude.[6] Since R. Dumont's famous warning about 'Black Africa's bad choice', to the present protests over the disastrous entry of our continent into economic globalisation and political internationalisation under the auspices of the United States, a series of studies has been conducted and similar calls been made for a radical change of course in Africa. Yet everything still gives the impression that the underlying problems have remained the same since independence.

On the political front, at the time when it was expected that the African people would free themselves from military dictatorships and their destructive systems, one was rather struck by the fact that the reasoning dominating the field of activity was not a structured plan to win decisive victories over ourselves and over destructive forces, nor was it the plan of a coherent and credible society, but rather, it consisted of nebulous strategies that had nothing to do with the current issues at stake, such as:

- strategies involving popular humour and mockery where we make fun of ourselves and our rulers so as to be able to bear the daily and unbearable pangs of reality;

- strategies of confrontation on unequal terms, where forces fighting for change were for years annihilated by military regimes;

- strategies of collaboration, compromise and shady deals which resulted in the addition of more years to the era of dictatorship;

- strategies of permanent improvisation, of crisis management and headlong flight without an in-depth analysis of long term objectives and without a societal plan that could radically change things.

Even where one had the impression that new forces had emerged and that an African rebirth was taking place, from Eritrea to Congo-Zaïre, one quickly realised, that the politico-military intelligence set in motion had suffered from the same inconsistency as the many internal struggles against dictatorships. Apart from the pseudo-revolutionary talk that characterised the power-hungry, there was nothing new in those who represented the dawn of a new Africa. There is a gulf of inconsistency between the problems, and the human resources needed to overcome them.[7]

Of course, there are instances where struggles have produced convincing and praiseworthy results. Some of these include Benin's democracy which is making progress, the experience of Mali's democratic struggle which looks promising, and South Africa which raises quite a lot of hope.

Should we for all this forget that in many African countries we are still struggling for the institution of democracy and a State where the laws of society are based on freedom and justice?

Our inconsistent action is even more evident here than anywhere else. Whereas the collapse of our economy with its subsequent difficulties called for strategies for local development and for the speeding up of African integration, as well as the unification of the continent's policies, everything today depends on rules and measures imposed by financial institutions whose priority objectives do not include the welfare of our countries.

The economic discussions on the need for integration impose this as the ultimate goal, at the time when the politics of privatisation is actually depriving Africa of its ability to take control of its economic destiny. Bound hand and foot, we enter into globalisation without a clear idea of what role we should play, without a vision of the human project we should champion, nor an effective understanding of the way we could influence its mechanisms to our advantage and fulfil the hopes of our people.

The same gap exists in relation to the mighty forces of our culture that we always invoke verbally and in incantations, without embodying them in strategies for social transformation and large-scale visible socio-political commitment. We have made such a folklore out of African culture that, in the end, what can be considered as 'the essence of its essence', that is, its creative force, has eluded us. Those who invoke it often only think of its remnants in plastic arts, songs, dances or even liturgical symbols which have parallels in Christian symbolism, without recognising that what is more important is the ability of that culture to produce a present and a future worthy of our humanity.

Destroying our sense of self-worth

Having reached this stage of our analysis, let us consider lucidly the problem of the destruction of our self worth. What underlies the insignificance of our being and our failure to make much impact, is the loss of meaning for our lives as peoples, cultures and civilisations. We have belittled, devalued and 'demonetised' ourselves, so to speak, by ceasing to believe in our own inner strengths and creative capabilities for building the future. In the scientific, economic, political, cultural or military domains, we have not given any credible indication that our search is guided by the desire to exploit our own resources and propose them as a way of life to the whole contemporary world. It is as if we did not value ourselves as human beings and as if we had even lost our ability to be human, that is, to be creators of the future.

When a people exhibits such a lack of faith in their own worth, they devalue themselves and are reduced to an inferior status where they receive and do not give in return. This gives others the impression that they have nothing to offer or that what they have to give is so insignificant that it does not add any value to their presence in the world. We are experiencing this situation today, and it can, to a large extent, negatively affect our ability to relate with other cultures.

In our research at the Academy of African Thought, as well as in the SCAT Academy, we were also struck by strategies in popular circles which belittle us. The predominance of the informal sector and an economy based on resourcefulness seems to have become the only visible answer our people have to the crisis, particularly in these times, as we enter a new millennium, when all countries are expected to provide ambitious answers that will transform their destiny.

Politically, in many countries, we are beginning to get used to sham democracies and rigged elections, the results of which are often contested without any drastic change. One also gets used to social violence and ethnic conflicts, as if we lack internal weapons against these ills. By force of habit, people cease to believe in the national and continental aspect of development, and confine themselves to the ethnic and tribal identity as the last resort: 'the little nigger strategy'.

All this shows that in the very imagination of the people, we are far from a collective momentum capable of forcing open the doors of destiny, and building the new society we all need.

Basic structure of the crisis of being in Africa

The preceding argument in this chapter on the African 'intelligence crisis' can be called into question if we decide to consider the problem from the point of view, not of the Africa in crisis, but of the Africa 'that forges ahead and wins'[8], the Africa whose positive experiences today present the image of immense hope. As Pierre Merli rightly points out in his book, *Espoir pour l'Afrique*[9] [*Hope for Africa*], there is no field of human endeavour in which events today do not show that Africa is moving forward.

We can, of course, find in all fields of endeavour, examples that could invalidate the generally pessimistic view we have of Africa since independence. In politics there have been not only Sékou Touré, Mobutu Sese Seko, Idi Amin Dada, Jean-Bédel Bokassa or Macias Nguéma, who were, in fact, pitiful caricatures of African power; there have also been many more African leaders of contrasting character such as Alphonse Massamba-Debat, Barthélemy Boganda, Léopold Sédar Senghor, Félix Houphouët-Boigny, Kwame Nkrumah and Julius Nyerere: a fine array of statesmen who can still inspire the present generation in their effort to envision the future and change our destiny.

In the economic field for a decade now, the image portrayed is that of Africa's growth characterised by a strong will and desire for success. This growth is not a product of a hyper-sensitive withdrawal into oneself, nor a fearful evasion of all the stakes of globalisation, but rather creates new entrepreneurs, new economic thinkers and new visionaries who give rise to great and lively hope everywhere. Although state-controlled economies are in chronic crisis, as is the case in many Central African countries, the economies of West and Southern Africa are vibrant and, indeed, promising.

Similarly, popular imagination is not an imagination in retreat. Civil society is bubbling with ideas and fresh impetus on human rights, conflict management, and education for public awareness. People are doing all they can to get themselves organised and to establish associations, movements and non-governmental bodies. Churches are becoming vigorously aware of their social responsibilities and are participating in the struggle for democracy, development and human improvement.

Instead of stubbornly clinging to a pessimistic perception of the African situation, one should rather read the signs of the times correctly and have an optimistic view of Africa; and even though the general impression given by Africa of itself after independence is disturbing, the nuances one can add today are such that the lucid analysis required should remain as close as possible to all the realities.

It is this requirement which we want to take into account at this second stage of our analysis. Some advice from Achille Mbembe will serve here as an introduction. When asked about the proper attitude to take with regard to the afro-pessimism and the afro-optimism that divide African researchers, the Cameroonian political scientist gave the following wise and perceptive answer:

> What you refer to as afro-pessimism and afro-optimism are basically an unfortunate oversimplification. No credit should be given to either of them. Nevertheless, two things come to mind. On the one hand, there is the real fact by which the continent's political, social, economic and cultural transformation processes are very much differentiated from each other. These transformational processes sometimes similar and at other times confused, are identical neither in their nature, form, quality, nor in their initial results. This complexity and these forms of confusion are enough to preclude any oversimplification of the African situation.[10]

After acknowledging this complexity, Achille Mbembe suggests a new perspective:

> At another level, the continent continues its sometimes traumatic, sometimes polemic, relationship with the world. We must get away from this situation where further progress is impossible. It is not a question of denying violence against Africa by external forces. It was and is still real, and often, it is done with the active complicity of local agents. But reasoning has to be carried a step further.

What does 'a step further' mean? Not towards an African identity 'expressed under the guise of restoring traditions', but to take control over the complex nature of life's processes in current African societies, their diffusion in the various diaspora, and in their ability to think about their plurality in order to offer a new vision of cosmopolitanism. 'Based on our experience and our history, we should review the very idea of cosmopolitanism'.

In the light of these considerations, it appears that the real problem is not that of being pessimistic or optimistic about the future of Africa, but of understanding our self-consciousness in order to act on it and thus release the innovation and dynamism which enrich us and could also enrich humanity as a whole. But what are the real dynamics of our consciousness as a people in search of a future? What do pessimism and optimism which are interwoven in our minds enable us to say clearly about our destiny ?

Our answer to this question is neither afro-pessimism nor afro-optimism but afro-lucidity, namely, the awareness of major obstacles against which we must fight to build the future. What is the content of the afro-lucid consciousness today? What form does it take and what are its requirements?

From the theoretical point of view, every social consciousness unfolds in three systems of reality with in-built active principles:

- the system of desire, or all the basic urges which govern a community's or society's relationship with possessions, and resolves all problems based upon this relationship, the value it confers, the social importance one acquires, the ambitions it generates and the moral authority it imposes;

- the system of knowledge which includes all means of apprehension and understanding of reality, the essential images, the basic logic, meaningful symbols and prerequisites which determine the intelligibility of the real and the composition of the scope of truth within which assertions become valid;

- the system of action: all practices relating to the transformation of the real and its compliance with the dreams and expectations of the society.

When we examine the afro-lucid consciousness in the light of the correlation established by these systems, or place it in the wider dimensions revealed by the theoretical works devoted to it, we then see that underlying afro-pessimism and afro-optimism are three types of dictatorship.

- There is the dictatorship of 'the belly' as the pivot of our desire, in an environment of scarcity and precariousness which impose social attitudes that condone a system of production and distribution of goods in a political economy of inequality, corruption, a scramble for the 'national cake', theft and embezzlement. This is apparently a system of existence which has nothing to do with the ethics of normal life. As Jean-François Bayart and Achille Mbembe[11] have demonstrated, in their publications on politics and African Christianity, respectively, since the early 1980s, the 'quest for wealth' constitutes a rich socio-philosophical and political concept for grasping the collective imagination in Africa. It determines and structures our social consciousness with such power that it makes men and women accept the unacceptable: the rule of triviality, inconsistency and the devaluation of oneself.

- There is also the dictatorship of alienation as the centre of our system of knowledge: with what logical and symbolic instruments do we establish our relationship with the world today? Where do we get the world view and global images which, to a large extent, condition our perception of ourselves and of our vision of the future?

Certainly they do not derive from an internal centre of gravity that would enable us to take charge of the major decisions through which we would get to grips with the world and change it, but from numerous external factors which condition us thoroughly. The world we should know, desire, love or build, is already determined by the era and environment within which we think about it: the era and environment of ultra-liberal magnetism in a cut-throat globalisation process, which promotes itself through images, representations and theories originating from the American way of life or from the policies of major financial institutions. It is as if, lacking the impetus for credible alternatives in images, representations and global theories, we have become content with alienation and have decided to believe that there is no other possible world than the ultra-liberal world which is built for us with its own source of power, domineering ambitions, powerful instincts and prospects for the dehumanisation of the planet through the logic of brute force.

- the dictatorship of powerlessness as the centre of our system of action; our inertia that keeps us from being the focal point of our own world; our powerlessness to create other world perspectives than those that reality has imposed on us as a way of life, and our powerlessness to act with all our strength in order to change our destiny.

As principles for the structuring of our social consciousness, the dictatorships of the belly, of alienation and powerlessness, are the arena from which the struggle for the future must begin. What is at stake, is changing these realities and introducing a new way of thinking, to promote an 'Africa' which is responsible for its own destiny. It is neither optimism nor pessimism but a desire for hope in the building of a new society.

Footnotes

[1] Michel Crozier, *La crise de l'intelligence* (Paris: Inter Editions, 1996), 183.

[2] I have borrowed this expression from Pascal Fossouo, a Cameroonian theologian who has made the focus of his study of inculturation of Christian faith, the chiefdoms of the west province of Cameroon.

[3] A. Mbembe, 'Il nous faut revaloriser la vie', an interview in *L'autre Afrique*, No. 71, 9-15 December 1998.

[4] We make reference here to the research work of the Guinean Jean Tounkara on modern African political systems and to the anthropology of the popular imagination developed by the Congolese scholar, Camille Kuyu. Both researchers undertook their research within the framework of the legal anthropology laboratory of the Sorbonne, in Paris.

5 A. Fantouré, *Le cercle des tropiques* (Paris: Présence Africaine, 1972); A. Kourouma, *Le soleil des indépendances* (Paris: Seuil, 1968); *En attendant le vote des bêtes sauvages* (Paris: Seuil, 1997); P. Ngandu-Nkashama, *Le pacte de sang* (Paris: l'Harmattan, 1978).

In Fantouré's novel, the ridiculous nature of African neo-colonial power is highlighted by a weird and incoherent character who imposes an insane and inhuman ideology on a people who accept subjection without realising that they are endangering their future. Those who fight against the imposed dictatorial power will, in the end, after a short and insignificant victory, be wiped out, as victims of an evil power revived from its own ashes.

Kourouma describes that power with all its tragi-comic attributes like the madness of words which mean nothing good, and of actions which produce nothing creative. African independence is characterised by fields littered with corpses and by desolation.

With Ngandu-Nkashama, desolation reaches absurdity: there is no hope, no future, no expectation. Dictatorship constitutes a serious obstacle to the future in a debauchery of madness, nonsense and absolute dehumanisation. Behind characters from novels, one easily recognises Mobutu, Eyadéma, Sékou Touré and many others.

6 We should point out as examples : F. Eboussi Boulaga, *La crise du Muntu* (Paris: Présence Africaine, 1977); P. Hountondji, *Sur la philosophie africaine* (Paris: Maspéro, 1978);J.-M. Elà, *Ma foi d'Africain* (Paris: Karthala, 1985); D. Etounga-Manguele, *L'Afrique a-t-elle besoin d'un programme d'ajustement culturel?* (Paris, Nouvelles du Sud, 1991); Beange Bolya, *L'Afrique en kimono* (Paris: Nouvelles du Sud, 1991); Kä Mana, *L'Afrique va-t-elle mourir?* (Paris: Karthala, 1991); Axelle Kabou, *Et si l'Afrique refusait le déoéloppement?* (Paris: l'Harmattan, 1991).

7 Hopes raised by Afeworki in Eritrea, Zenawi in Ethiopia, Museveni in Uganda, Kagamé in Rwanda and Kabila in Democratic Republic of Congo, quickly proved to be illusive and hollow: a road that leads nowhere!

8 The words of a French researcher, Philippe Engelhardt, now working in Dakar, at ENDA-Tiers-Monde. He devotes his analysis to the experiences of Africa that forge ahead, in order to lay the basis for his main thesis: 'the next century will belong to Africa'. M. Engelhardt shared his thoughts with us during the Ecumenical meeting organised in 1994 in Senegal, by Afrique-Avenir Panafrican Protestant Foundation. Addressing young people who gathered there on that occasion, Philippe Engelhardt suggested essential keys that could enable Africa to take on its destiny in the next millennium: faith in oneself, courage to think big, promotion of human values and the sense of a rational organisation of things.

[9] A book published by Présence Africaine, Paris, 1990.

[10] A. Mbembe, *Il nous faut revaloriser la vie*.

[11] Cf. J. F. Bayart, *L'Etat en Afrique, la politique du ventre* (Paris: Fayard, 1989); J. F. Bayart et al, *La politique par le bas en Afrique noire* (Paris: Karthala, 1998); A. Mbembe, *Afriques indociles* (Paris: Karthala, 1989).

CHAPTER 3

Rebuilding our existence

After our analyses of the global situation against which there is an urgent need for society to fight, we deemed it necessary to extend the scope of research to cover the requirements needed to overcome the crisis.

The main trend of the Academy of African Thought, like that of the SCAT Academy, was to try to rebuild the entire African existence, value and action on solid foundations. As Professor Fabien Kange Ewane says, 'It is necessary to get out of the traps of others into which we have fallen, in order to be reconciled with the depths of our own vital energy, culture, and the underlying forces of our civilisation'. To quote Mrs. A. Traoré in her essay, 'L'étau',[1] 'It is above all necessary to break loose from the stranglehold upon our destiny and thus build a new society'.

Getting out of the trap, breaking loose from the stranglehold

This requirement expresses first an obvious fact which has been repeated in African thought for many years, like an incantatory ritual, an argument full of boring slogans in which nothing new appears under the black tropical sun. The most important thing is for us not to allow ourselves to be convinced, dominated, and guided by what the most recent centuries of our history have done to us, from the slave trade right to the current ultra-liberal globalisation.

Nonetheless, behind this obvious truth is a radical requirement for every African today: a need to fight with all our strength against our insignificance, our inconsistency and our ontological debasement of ourselves, in order to build a new society devoid of the dictatorships of the 'belly', alienation and powerlessness. We cannot really succeed in such a struggle, if, as F. Kange Ewane says, we continue to see ourselves through the eyes of others, to measure ourselves by the standards of others and to act with the resources of others, without asking ourselves basic questions about the consequences of such a situation for our future. We cannot fashion a new destiny either, if, as Mrs Traoré states emphatically, we do not take control of our creative power of imagination.

From the time of launching the Negritude Movement in the 1930s, to the current politico-social movement of African renaissance, which has been given impetus by the South African President, Thabo Mbeki, with, in-between, the era of ideologies of the African personality or the 'farce' of Zairean authenticity (as U. Y. Mudimbe would say), we have all felt in Africa that this is a crucial problem for our continent.

Rather than continue to suffer the torments of the deadly stranglehold and to remain in a trap set by others, we have understood that we should break loose and promote a new consciousness based on what we really are. It is here that the decisive question emerges: Who are we, basically? What do we really represent? What are the bases of our being and where are the origins of our destiny?

For historians of our two academies, there is no doubt that the central drive of our cultural, human and vital strength emanates from pharaonic Egypt, the place which gave rise to the spirit and intellect of black civilisations. From this source, a heritage of vital thought has been fashioned in African history, based on its treasures, knowledge, wisdom and manner of living, a heritage which constitutes an essence of existence we refer to by the generic term of African traditions. Our existence depends on these traditions which enrich our creative powers. Thinking about this relationship with ourselves and a new imagination of our destiny, is an imperative from which we cannot escape.

F. Kange Ewane and G. Bilolo Mubabinge are of the view that having been plunged by the circumstances of history into the trap of others, we have been severed from two sources of creativity, namely, ancient Egypt and African traditions. Once detached from these two vital sources, we no longer have a soul, life and a creative spirit as a people, a culture or civilisation. We can only become shallow people, without the basic formative logic or solid principles of action and only be dominated spiritually, religiously, politically, economically and militarily. Exhausted beings without their creative spirit can only become people without any power of historical initiative. Such is the source of our powerlessness, inconsistency and debasement of our existential worth.

Though contemporary African thought has for a long time been aware of this problem, not all the political, economic, pedagogic, moral, spiritual and military lessons have yet been drawn from it. The advent of a new century, which we hope will be the century of Africa, will compel us to re-examine this problem: to think again about this

'common place' of our current society according to truly new theoretical and practical perspectives.

Beginning the struggle for rebuilding our existence

The problem of rebuilding our existence by rediscovering ancient
Egypt and vital African traditions, thus appeared to us in its true
dimensions. It is not a question of ideological and political entertain-
ment as was the case with the policy of authenticity in Zaïre during
the time of Mobutu Sese Seko; nor is it a question of asserting
ourselves as human beings in the quest for recognition by the other
world, the West, the white world, as imagined by the founders of
Negritude and advocates of African personality. Rather it is a need to
fight seriously against our own ontological decline, as Bilolo
Mubabinge would say, or our anthropological poverty, according to
the well-known expression of Engelbert Mveng.[2] It is a question of
arming ourselves with the only weapons that matter today in order
to overcome worthlessness, inconsistency and the debasement of our
spirit.

These weapons are essentially the regrafting of our inner selves
onto our vital sources of power, and appropriating once again our
powers of initiative, in order to restructure our being in preparation
for the struggles of today, to conduct our activity in a creative manner
and to build the future society on life-promoting thoughts.

To define better the content of this existential problem, we set
ourselves to interrogate the wisdom of our fathers, which is still available to us today:

- the philosophical cosmo-theologies of ancient Egypt (Bilolo
Mubabinge's scope of research and the African research teams he
leads);

- the foundation myths of African human existence in major black
esoteric traditions (the specialisation of Professor Essoh Ngome and
his research groups);

- legends, narratives and traditions through which the elders in
our villages maintain our cultural heritage (area of reflection and
action of Professor Kange Ewane);

- African popular imagination in its rooting in the heart of African
traditions (an area where we are carrying out research ourselves into
the struggle against powerlessness, inconsistency and the debasement
of the African being).

To conduct our research and co-ordinate our activities in the two
academies, we devised a work methodology:

- collect cosmogonies, myths, epics and legends on the origins of our being from several African cultures;

- determine their hermeneutical usefulness in relation to the problem of the meaning of our life and the significance of our destiny;

- compare their basic structures with those of the myths of other peoples by referring to research already undertaken by western ethnology;

- draw up a global theory of the basis of African culture and its fruitfulness in solving the problems of present-day Africa.

Given the great number of narratives, legends and cosmogonies at our disposal, we found it helpful to select the following three myths from which to examine the problem of salvation as the basis of our being:[3]

- the Egyptian narrative of Isis and Osiris as a manifestation of a state of society and perennial problems of relationship between human beings;

- the myth of the separation of God and humankind as a perceived order of reality in a society whose original values constitute the basis of the human;

- the myth of the creation of the world and human beings as a theoretical tentative foundation of existence and reality as they are today, and as they demand from humanity - a concrete commitment to the promotion of life.

In these three myths, we set out to view African humanism as an essential locus for the search for meaning,[4] an arena of life and action where dialogue with Jesus Christ offers to Africa new possibilities for the struggle against the powerlessness of our being, the inconsistency of our action and the devaluation of our presence in the world of today.

Footnotes

[1] A. Traoré, *L'étau* (Paris: Actes Sud, 1998).

[2] Of interest are: Bilolo Mubabinge, *Les cosmo-théologies philosophiques de l'Egypte antique* (Kinshasa-Libreville-Munich: Publications Universitaires Africaines, 1986); Engelbert Mveng, *Théologie, liberation and cultures africaines* (Yaoundé/Paris: Clé/Présence Africaine, 1996).

[3] Here we study myth in its essential meaning as a global system of 'religious or metaphysical beliefs', vital convictions in general, in which 'social order and the order of things can be united into one whole by reference to origins that date back before the emergence of evil or to the final destiny beyond death' (Edition Ortigues, quoted by L.-V. Thomas and R. Luneau in their famous book, *La terre*

africaine et ses religions (Paris: L'Harmattan, 2nd edition, 1995).

[4] Myth is perceived here as the expression of a sacred tradition which cannot be reduced or confined to a fixed meaning according to a single, eternal and unchanging norm from the creation of the world to the end of time. It refers instead to superabundance of meaning where the period of origins, even though included in 'bodies of beliefs, ritual systems, daily activities and even the mode of production' typical of a specific social system, still constitutes an important point of departure for new possibilities of being and new prospects of self-creation in new contexts of life (cf. L.-V. Thomas and R. Luneau, *La terre africaine*).

CHAPTER 4

Isis, Osiris and Jesus Christ

From the 'sarcophagus principle' to the 'power of the cross'

The main outline of the myth of Isis and Osiris should first be recalled here before giving it a christological meaning in the context of the problem of salvation in the present situation of the African continent.

Osiris, a one time Pharoah, reigned over the prosperous kingdom of Egypt. His wife was his sister, Isis, who helped him rule the kingdom and establish its influence.

Osiris's brother, Seth, coveted the Pharoah's power and hatched a plot against him. He made a beautiful sarcophagus and presented it to all the dignatories of the kingdom during a big festival, claiming that he would present this splendid and incomparable jewel to anyone whose measurements would fit the dimensions of the sarcophagus.

This was a trap for Osiris. After managing to convince him to lie in the sarcophagus, Seth then skillfully followed his pre-meditated plan, shut the sarcophagus, had it locked with huge padlocks and threw it in the marsh; after which he seized power.

Isis, now a widow, started looking for the corpse of her husband-brother. Following reports from the court, she found the sarcophagus, took out her brother's corpse and buried it with dignity and honour.

While wandering in the marsh one day, Seth discovered the empty sarcophagus. He mounted a search for Osiris's corpse, found it, and cut it into pieces; after which he scattered the pieces over the Nile.

Isis once again began looking for the scattered pieces of her husband-brother. When she found them, she gathered the pieces, made a male sex organ, and stuck it to Osiris's patched up corpse. With the help of this organ, she made herself pregnant and gave birth to a son: Horus.

When Horus became an adult, he avenged the death of his father,

Osiris, by seizing the power that his uncle had usurped.

This myth would seem to have no christological dimension, and nothing to do with theological research in the area of Christian faith. Yet in giving it a social interpretation, Professor Essoh Ngome notes that 'things change completely if one considers the whole myth from the point of view of Africa in quest of her destiny and salvation in the world. Africa, not as it was in the past, but as it is today'.

Osiris would stand for the sublime and grandiose image that Africa has of its past, its creative forces, its vital strengths and its inventive powers. He is the symbol of a lost prosperity and vanished greatness.

After being locked up in the colonial sarcophagus, which represents both the immobility of non-being and the inertia of all creative forces, Africa was then dislocated and dismembered at the time of independence, by the forces of demolition and various economic and socio-political powers, which are symbolised by Seth. This is Africa, suffering every misfortune and all kinds of catastrophes, hardships and despair.

Economically, politically, culturally, socially, ethically and spiritually, it lies in the shackles of a dark destiny, and is locked in a non-sense empire, an irreparable non-life.

Isis represents all the cultural forces that accept neither the immobility of the non-being, the inertia of the non-sense, nor the fatality of the non-life. She is the centre of creative forces linked to anthropological, ontological and social solidarity, symbolised here by the marriage bond between brother and sister. She represents the rigorous and patient quest for ways out of the non-life. She is the liberator, the willpower for creative freedom which should ensure the breaking of the sarcophagus into pieces and thus the restoration of some dignity to Africa despite its misfortune.

After Seth's heinous crime - the symbol of the forces of the dislocation, destruction, dissipation and annihilation of the powers of life - Isis appears as the one who gathers, integrates, 'panafricanises' and, above all, gives a new creative power through the sex organ she herself makes.

This male symbol through which the dead regains its ability to impregnate a woman, shows Isis's power and creative intellect. She appears not only as a person, but as a group of researchers involved in the search for solutions to overcome non-sense, non-life and non-being.

From Isis's impregnation by Osiris whose dismembered body is patched up again and sexually reconstituted, Horus is born; Horus, the symbol of a new Africa, one which opens up a new destiny and starts a merciless, ruthless fight against the forces of destruction and demolition.

This Africa defeats all forces that had sought to annihilate its power to initiate in history.

It is helpful to realise that in the myth, the birth of a new Africa is linked with the enrichment of the spirit of research typified by Isis, through the powers available in the culture, embodied in Osiris, and brought together and revitalised.

According to Professor Essoh Ngome's interpretation of the myth, Africa has in itself the powers of rebirth, revitalisation and resumption of its historical initiative.

Starting from the certitude and conviction that the myth of Isis and Osiris takes us to the roots of African culture, what kind of christology can be envisioned where Christ's personality is accepted, re-examined, re-interpreted, re-imagined and rooted deeply in the mythological framework of our vision of the world?

How does Christ's personality become important, useful, necessary and fruitful, in problems related to the sense of worthlessness of our being, the inconsistency of our action and the devaluation of our vital powers?

The sarcophagus and the cross: two principles of life

Let us first be clear on this point. In as much as our relationship to the myth is fulfilled through the recapture of the entire meaning that would give weight and significance to our lives, that relationship cannot be reduced to merely the fruitful elements that we need here and now. The meaning we get from it today can become pertinent and fruitful, only if it does not close in on itself by becoming an opaque totality. That meaning might merely become a new sarcophagus.

To avoid that risk, it is necessary to have both an internal and external power which can 'break down' the false 'totality of meaning' to which the myth could be reduced. If the myth constitutes food for thought, to borrow the famous expression of Paul Ricœur, someone else must really make us see and understand it, by breaking the conceptual shackles which prevent us from getting into its 'super-abundance of meaning', that wealth which constitutes the very greatness of the narratives, which form the basis of our being and existence.

In the interpretation of the myth of Isis and Osiris, the cross of Christ would represent that unknown perspective, which opens new possibilities of understanding the very dynamism of the myth in its manifold semantic senses.

Together with a group of young intellectuals involved in theological reflection on Africa, we undertook research with the aim of viewing christology in the light of the results of the African study of the myths of ancient Egypt, and of opening up ways to the new meaning which the personality of Jesus could have within the heart of our 'grove of initiation'.

The guiding principle in this research is to show that, at the level of the underlying myths which enrich social imagination, possibilities do exist today for integrating Christ in the cultural and spiritual re-establishment of destiny, that is, in our quest for salvation. It is therefore necessary to think about Christ from a mythological perspective where he represents a revitalising power of our divided and dislocated Africa, in order to give back to our continent its capacity to create a new life, out of all the sarcophaguses that suffocate and kill us.

At the mythological heart of African existence, this Christ acts as a force springing from the depths of our own African cultural powers, to enrich our creative intellect. It is also a force that derives from the transcendent realm as well as coming through the historical trajectory of the western world, to penetrate our minds and increase our resourcefulness in the quest to liberate the future.

This dual image of Christ as the inner illuminator, on the one hand, and, on the other, as an external motivator and re-creative otherness, leads us to an understanding of his destiny and message from the very perspective of the mythological origins of existence. He is an initiatory figure[1] who illuminates the spirit of the mythological origins of our culture, and who shows that the salvation of the African continent, that is, the building of a new society, depends on the fruitful cross-fertilisation between a lucid observation of our culture where Christian faith had its origin, and divine-historical exteriority, from where it comes to Africa in the form of a message that enriches, 'detotalises' our interpretations of our own being, and opens up new directions.[2]

What does Christ stand for in his capacity as a lucid observer of the inner cultural workings of Africa, that is, in the interpretation that Africa would give of the forces that destroy her ? Christ cannot appear as the way of salvation, merely to bring to light the underlying elements which the Isis and Osiris myth discloses, and which Professor Essoh Ngome's interpretation has brought to light. He enters our grove to make us see what our immediate interests do not allow us to see.

We see, first of all, our collective fascination in the face of the many political, economic, social, cultural, religious and spiritual sarcophaguses, which forces of domination and enslavement use to attract, entice and seduce us as ways to happiness, whilst in reality, their only aim is to dispossess us of our freedom, creativity and power of historical initiative. From the foundations of our culture and the very spirit of our civilisation, we are swept along pathologically in a vision where the sarcophagus is an essential symbol - the symbol of the attempt to dispossess us of our responsibility as historical actors and makers of our own history, to the advantage of all sorts of usurpers who claim to wish us well, but who are really burying us in exquisite coffins where we may sleep quietly for ever.

Second, we see fratricidal violence as an element inherent in culture and in its basic mechanisms. Violence reveals itself not only in political institutions and in the higher realms of power, but also in everyday relationships where social groups, communities or ethnic groups, base their relationships with others on the principles of exclusion and the extermination of all who are different. This results in the denial of basic human rights, and in the dehumanisation of other persons by reducing them to the state of beasts of burden, a commodity or nothing at all.

Third, we perceive revenge instincts, which characterise the forces that overthrow political regimes, based on a logic that does not mean that a change of political regime transforms the standards of living of the people in general.

Finally we discern social relationships based on an indescribable jumble of lies, deceit and all kinds of sham, where one wonders whether words like 'truth' and 'human consideration' have any meaning at all.

Faced with these elements of the myth, Christ may be seen as a creative force in several ways.

-He is the anti-sarcophagus principle par excellence: the refusal to let oneself be fascinated by all who want to build our happiness for us, at the expense of our freedom and dignity, at the expense, above all, of our responsibility in confronting the future, and at the expense of our power of historical initiative. It is a question in fact, of a complete change of mind, by which we do not allow a society to become a sarcophagus space in which relationships are devoid of all their potential for creativity, and all their possibilities of truly rooting people in the humane.

-He embodies the ability to re-establish the shattered fraternity between Osiris and his brother through the invention of a new fraternity that takes in Africa and humanity as a whole, a new spiritual fabric of brotherly and sisterly relationships in Christ. In Christ, the brother and the sister are not given to me through the simple bond of blood or through the fact that we live on the same piece of land,[3] they are created by the spirit of God and placed in a living space called 'culture of neighbourliness', 'civilisation of brotherhood'. These expressions must be understood with the same connotations and the same resonances as those we use when we speak about 'business culture' or 'universal civilisation'.

-He reveals the possibility of a life of conciliation and reconciliation that does not use violence, nor extols the will to power, but which asserts itself in absolute self-denial: the way of the cross.

This way is that of a 'culture of service' and of a 'civilisation based on active solidarity', where power is not asserted on mainly hierarchical and pharaonic political imperatives, but on the requirements of a social order where all citizens are strongly bound together in a common conquest of happiness through justice and freedom.[4]

-He enables the orientation of spiritual and cultural creativity towards the ethics of true being of where individual and social existence are guided by the values of the availability of oneself to the other.

Christ is incapable of being reduced to our inner cultural world, since he also comes to us as the absolute otherness of God, by means of another civilisation and in a powerful and rich dogmatic construct. We cannot but interpret the personality of Christ as the totality of external creative forces which consolidate and boost our own power of creativity and resourcefulness.

The revitalising and re-creative interiority of his personality in the mythical origins of our culture receives from his detotalising otherness and his enriching exteriority, a living impetus towards new forms of meaning.

From this perspective, two ideas deserve to be highlighted as a vital contribution of a christology of cultural rebirth and enrichment.

- The teaching of Christ is not only a manifestation of a God who is love according to the beautiful assertions of our Christian tradition and of our catechisms, but a God who is pure love, according to the wonderful new theological understanding which Father François Varillon has bequeathed to world Christianity, an understanding which we compare here with the bright idea of Father Jean Cardonnel recently brought to light by Father René Luneau: Jesus Christ as 'the only person who proclaimed God'[5] and who, by this very fact, enables us to see him purely in the light of a being who is pure love.

- The person, life, teaching and action of Jesus Christ are the revelation of the human in a dynamic permanent 'transformation' of people and society according to the beatitudes, that is, the total reversal of values towards the advent of a culture based on the integral meaning of humanity.

Beatitudes here refer to a general orientation of the mind to build a society whose main values are in accordance with God's plan, especially paying attention to the very poor, the destitute and the lowest, as theologians from Latin America have never ceased to expound in their well-known Theology of Liberation.[6]

If we consider these elements as an integral part of a new cultural foundation which is universal and which applies to all cultures and civilisations, we should realise that the personality of Christ constitutes a major basis for African cultural rebirth.

That is why Christ is the way to salvation: the opening of a new meaning in the very heart of culture,[7] of a new reality where Africans, rooted in their vital native land, and renewed in Jesus Christ, can in no way become insignificant, inconsistent and debased in their being.

To put it plainly, Christ is the one who saves us from our insignificance, inconsistency and loss of value, once we welcome him into the very heart of our culture as the fertile ground for our self-affirmation and our creativity.

Proclaiming God and humanising humans, he launches Africa on the path of reconstruction, building a new society. That is the way of salvation.

Footnotes

[1] On all these aspects, the book edited by F. Kabassele, Joseph Doré and René Luneau and entitled, *Chemin de la christologie africaine* (Paris: Desclée Publishers, 1986), will be of great interest. [Editor: Many of these essays are reproduced in English translation in Robert Schreiter (ed.), *Faces of Jesus in Africa* (Maryknoll: Orbis Books, 1991).]

[2] We have borrowed the terms 'totalisation' and 'detotalisation' from the Latin-American theologian, E. Dussel, in his book entitled *Ethique communautaire* (Paris: Cerf, 1991).

[3] On this point, we recommend our book, *Théologie africaine pour temps de crise* (Paris: Karthala, 1993).

[4] Cf. our commentary on pharaonism in our booklet, *Eglises africaines et théologies de la reconstruction* (Geneva: Protestant Centre for Studies, 1994).

[5] In his famous letters sent around the world entitled, *Afrique et parole*, Father Luneau announced in n° 53, December 1998, a book he intended to publish in March 1999 entitled, *Jésus, l'homme qui évangélisa Dieu*. He claims to have been inspired by a word from Father Jean Cardonnel: 'If I believe in Jesus Christ, it is because he is the only person to proclaim God'.

6 Cf. Clodovis Boff and Jorge Pixley, *Les pauvres: choix prioritaires* (Paris: Cerf, 1991); Ronaldo Munnoz, *Dieu: 'J'ai vu la misère de mon peuple'* (Paris: Cerf, 1992).

7 Father François Varillon has written in a stimulating manner on these topics in his book of lectures put together by Bernard Housset under the title, *Joie de vivre, joie de croire* (Paris: Le Centuron, 1981).

CHAPTER 5

The myth of the separation of men and the withdrawal of God

In our work with the Academy of African Thought and the SCAT Academy, our research deals not only with Egyptology, but also with cultural traditions in Africa, especially with the cosmogonic legends and the myth of creation where culture reveals its meaning and discloses its deep motivating forces.

From the point of view of the problem of salvation and its christological influence, a particular cosmogonic story has engaged our attention because of its significance: the myth of the withdrawal of God and the sharing of space among human beings.

First version of the myth

This myth has several versions. We shall first narrate the version of the Giziga in the northern part of Cameroon.[1]

> Once upon a time, heaven was near the earth and Bumbulvun lived with men. Heaven was so near that men had to stoop to walk; yet they did not have to worry about what to eat, they only had to stretch out their hands and tear off pieces of heaven for food.

> But one day, a young girl, a chief's daughter, who was a *mukuwan* (a naughty girl who did everything the wrong way and the opposite of what others did), instead of taking bits of the vault of heaven to feed on, started looking to the ground and choosing grains she found on the ground. Then she made herself a mortar and a pestle to grind the grains she chose.

> Each time she knelt down and raised her pestle, it would hit against heaven and also against God. Frustrated in her work, the young girl said to heaven, 'God, won't you move just a bit ?' Heaven moved a bit further, and the young girl was able to stand up. As she went on

and ground her grains, she raised her pestle still higher. Soon she
implored heaven for a second time; again heaven moved a bit
further. Then she began throwing her pestle up in the air. When she
asked a third time, heaven became outraged and moved far away to
its present location.

From that time on, men have been able to walk and stand up. They
no longer feed on pieces from heaven, but have become millet
eaters. In addition, God does not appear to men as he used to, long
ago, when every evening, he would come and act as their arbitra-
tor. Now men are left alone to settle their problems; hence there is
war.

Those who have previously commented on this myth, R. Jaouen,
L. V. Thomas and R. Luneau, have been very impressed with the
anthropological wealth and the great theological impact of the
thought it develops. They perceive in it the essential human issue:
freedom and responsibility as prerogatives for erect humans, called
upon to begin working so as not to live weighed down in the face of
transcendent forces: heaven, in all the suffocating power it represents.
   'God is so near that men can walk only by stooping.' There is plenty
of food but, we dare say, it is another instance of the 'alienation' of
human beings. They eat pieces of heaven, which has made them
perpetually 'assisted' persons. To conclude, there is no social life yet,
since God comes to settle problems. Strangely enough, this golden age
is that of a 'colonised land' where, apparently, 'only heaven gets something out of it'.[2]
   Whatever positive or negative way we perceive the young girl's
behaviour towards heaven, a radical break down of the human condition occurs through her attitude of mind, her rejection of the dictatorship of 'another' and of any life of submission to God that borders on
real slavery, even if this slavery has an exquisite side: material security.
   Breaking with such a condition, the young girl establishes a new
destiny for humankind: an existence which the Czech philosopher,
Jan Patocka, would refer to as the problem of existence,[3] the fact of
no longer relying on mythical or divine certainties, but rather relying
solely on the power of human reason and creativity. Even if the order
of human reason and creativity gives way to a permanent state of war,
the latter is preferable to slavery and submission. It is all the more
preferable because the discussion of problems always heralds victory
over warlike instincts, as one would put it.
   If the human order, such as freedom, responsibility and creativity,
always comes with conflict, if anthropology without theology leads to
a state of permanent antagonism and confrontation, the question to

ask immediately is how to manage society in a fruitful and peaceful way.

Second version of the myth

On this question, the version of the same myth among the Fang (Gabon, Equatorial Guinea) is very instructive. In his famous *Anthologie nègre*,[4] Blaise Cendrars reproduces the story under the title *La légende de la séparation*. Here is the essential storyline of that legend.

In the beginning, human beings lived together in the same village and were often visited by God. 'Peace reigned in the village and the Creator was happy.'

'But soon a dispute arose' when in their daily activities, the oldest women in the community became consistently engaged in conflicts with the youngest women. Solutions proposed by the men during a consultative assembly did not yield any results; the disputes persisted and society threatened to explode under the weight of the conflict.

Ndun, the wise old man who was responsible for relationships between human beings and God, consulted God on the issue. 'O God, Creator, Master of all, you made me chief of the village of men, that is good. You created men, that is also good! But, you created women, that is not good! Men live together in peace, but with women, peace is impossible. It is you who created us, it is you who must give us peace again. Women and porcupines are one and the same thing'.

God came down to earth with old Ndun. He observed the situation and thus addressed the human race: 'You have become too many to live on the same hill (...). You will thus part company. Some will go to the right, others to the left. Some will go forward, others will go backward, and so you will live in peace. Each group has to take animals along and settle in its own area.'

After calling the wise old man back to himself through death, God ordered that two women, one old and the other young, be sacrificed by the spilling of their blood. This was done and both women died. After their death, the Creator said: 'Dig a deep pit'. When it was dug, the Creator ordered, 'Put the wise old man at the bottom of the pit'. And when he had been put in the pit, the Creator said: 'Now, set the two women ablaze'. And they were burnt. Once this was done, the Creator announced, 'This is the sacrifice, and you will do this once more when I instruct you to. I am the Master'. The Creator ordered that some of the ashes of the two women be kept, and the rest of their ashes sprinkled on the body of the dead wise old man. This was to be accompanied by the singing of dirges.

After the sacrifice of the two women, the Creator ordered that a sacrifice of animals too be carried out. 'The blood of animals flowed, until it covered the entire hill.' Those who had no animals to sacrifice were asked to bring wood. Animals were placed on it. And, suddenly, what we now call 'fire' arose. The Creator made a sign, and thunder struck, and lightening flashed, and a huge flame arose immediately, and the wood started to burn. The men thus became of the same mind and the son of the dead wise old man started singing a song about fire.

After the animal sacrifice, people gathered the ashes of the animals and those of Ndun, the wise old man, 'each person their share, each person their part'. The Creator added, 'That is the covenant of the union'. And the men answered, 'We want it this way. We are brothers and we belong to one race'. Ashes were thrown on Ndun's corpse, a pit was dug, and was filled with ashes, and the Creator ordered that they should look for stones. These stones which were then placed on the pit rose higher and higher. The Creator said, 'This is the sign. When you are travelling and you see a place where a man is buried, you will throw either a stone, a branch or a leaf on it and you will do as I have asked'.

And when the pile of stones had risen higher and higher, the Creator said to the men, 'It is here that we must part company'. Men then started to leave, some to the right, others to the left, some going forward and others backwards, but nobody remained at that spot. This was the first event. Then came the second, at the point when men were about to separate. This is therefore the second thing that happened. The Creator said to men, 'It is finished. I will no longer take care of you'.

To those men who were complaining about this separation, he gave the assurance that the strong and powerful spirit of the race would be with them. He gave the last recommendation, that is, a ritual in which each person would mix his blood with that of an animal which would thus become his blood brother with a special virtue. 'And that is why w,e the Ndun, have the crocodile', concluded the myth.

An anthropological and philosophical interpretation

One does not need to be a great anthropologist to understand that this myth is really about the origins of humanity. The themes which feature in it centre on two things, the relationship between people in a society and the relationship between the society and God.

In the first problem, conflict as the basic dynamic of social life is brought to light, and the purpose of the whole story is to learn how to resolve it. God intervenes because of humanity's inability to find solutions to this problem. His lesson on separation will institute a global order where there will be principles guaranteed by a specific ritual. A creative word gives birth to an order of life based on a regulatory law. People share space and establish a covenant based on the sacrifice of what they have, something that is both very precious (the old wise man around whom everything centres) and most feared (woman as the source of conflict). We are given symbols of this covenant which is a covenant not just between people, but with an entire creation. A social global order is thus created, an order whose supreme regulator is the Creator. It is the order of a fraternity of the human race with the acceptance of God as Father.

According to the myth, this established fraternity is the basis of culture and the root of civilisation. It is this fraternity that gives meaning to the diversity of communities and ensures space and identity of each ethnic group. This fraternity is the source of the authentic human relationship between human beings and the harbinger of their collective destiny.

In addition to this original fraternity, there is an even more important theological reality, namely the death of theodicy, that is, of all relationship with God which would make God an ultimate providence, ever ready to intervene in human affairs.[5] As guarantor of divine centralism, of a supernatural dictatorship and the fear of the sacred, the Almighty God whom one could call upon at any time to govern and direct all through everlasting power and terrorising of minds, would no longer have any place at the heart of society. To be more exact, the very one who emphatically said, 'I am the Master', now relinquished his power in order to give men their liberty. 'It is finished. I will no longer be responsible for you'. This is the beginning of an order based on responsibility and community freedom which people themselves must exercise, according to the principles of sacrifice and covenant. This death of theodicy is as basic as the fraternity of the human race. Once God has allocated space among social groups and established rules and rites to structure collective life, he no longer has any place as master of this space. He withdraws and distances himself. Human order thus becomes established and developed on the basis of this withdrawal.

From these two basic elements, we can conclude that the search for the meaning of existence which troubles the minds of people, is driven by the need to build a society based on brotherhood and responsibility, where each person, each social group, each tribe and each ethnic group has the duty to renew itself at the height of its own actual reality, that is, from the source of culture itself, namely where God establishes humankind and withdraws. The meaning thus given to the higher collective destiny becomes a structuring principle on which life is built and developed. Since God gave humanity its protocols and norms, it is up to human beings to take over their humanity and enrich their existence here and now. In fact, the entire myth of separation seems to bring to light essential principles in the foundation of African culture.

The first principle concerns the transition from theodicy to anthropology. Central African traditions define this by the expression 'Zo kue zo' meaning 'any human being is a human being'. 'Any human person is a human person'. Every man and woman has his or her being rooted in a common sphere of a shared humanity. No person should, under any pretext, be taken out of this space and buried in a type of subhumanity or superhumanity. A person (or a group, in this case, women) who becomes a disturbing element in the collective space, does not however cease to be a human being, but should be brought back into the common order of being through the requirements of the gift of self (symbolised by sacrifice) and responsible solidarity (symbolised by the relationship with God, or else the ancestor).

The second principle is that of theological ontology which makes the respect for human rights the absolute basis. The Baluba of Congo-Kinshasa describe it by the expression, 'Man is God's other person'. His being consists in belonging to another person who belongs to God. The meaning of his existence lies in the development of this ontology of the primordial relation, which links it to others as mediation towards the Creator, towards God.

The third principle refers to a requirement in a love relationship and means 'to hold firmly together', as the Bassa people of Cameroon put it. To hold firmly together in the human, this spirit of the race which the story of separation talks about; hold firmly together to the advice, which the Creator left before going back to his own realm; hold themselves together to develop the domain where God sent each group, in order to avoid any fratricidal conflict.

In the theological research being undertaken in the Academy of African Thought and the SCAT Academy, it is within the vital area carved out by these principles that it is helpful to develop a christology of the encounter between Africa and Jesus Christ in the 'grove of initiation', as christology that has significance for the quest for salvation, that is, for meaning as the creative dynamics of humanity and promoter of harmony in relationships. Insofar as successful relationship is the very basis of humanity, salvation means making persons capable of freeing themselves from the dictates of insignificance, the despotism of weakness, and the anthropological catastrophe of debasing themselves through the very fervour that leads them to more fruitful human relationships with others.

Christological perspective

How do we situate Christ here? What role do we assign to him? We can attempt to answer the first question in the following terms: Insofar as he is an absolute otherness and a de-totalising exteriority, which calls into question the temptation of reductionism where we think we can exhaust the meaning of our own creation myths, Christ comes into our 'grove' to open our eyes to what we do not see. In the myth concerning the separation of human beings and the withdrawal of God, the figure of Christ reveals what is hidden in it: the extremism of a principle of separation where Africa has made use of the reality of ethnic differences to make each community a principle of exclusivism and aggressive seclusion. The Rwandan genocide bore all the hallmarks of horror and cruelty inherent in such a principle.

Where the founding order of African humanism operated on a vision of society based on equitable sharing of space, property and possibilities for fulfilment, we have brought in ethnocentrism, ethnic wars and a most despicable racism. We have gone against the word of our ancestors by going to the extreme of adopting a culture of destroying the other person, reducing him to a sub-human, if not a non-human, status.

Christ shows at the heart of our grove that the worm was in the very fruit of the principle of separation, insofar as this principle introduced an order based on soil and blood, on totemic identification in a territory given to a social group united to an Ancestor, forgetting the law of the Creator who, nonetheless, is as real as the common Father.

In Christ, a new principle of identification by reference to the 'Father' is established: the one identified as Father of all human beings cannot be reduced to a totem or to a protecting ancestor. He is referred to as the Spirit in a broader sense than that of the spirit of the race the myth speaks about. He is the Spirit of the human: the new seed of the divine in any person, in any people, in any culture, and in any civilisation. He is not concerned with 'uniting' through soil and blood, but in liberating through the spirit, as we have already seen in the previous myth. The breath of universal brotherhood springs forth from him to a world given over to the demons of separatism.

With the Father as revealed by Jesus, we grasp clearly the dangers, threats and damaging effects of the petty principles of our ethnic exclusivism. We enter the vast human project whose gospel represents the main principle: conversion to the Spirit of God who makes every person a human being, an absolute, before whom I have no other duty than to show love, no other rights than to be loved by him in the breath of the Spirit.

Another reality which Christ reveals in the heart of our grove of initiation, is the latent universal violence which René Girard referred to as the 'victimising mechanism', and the logic of the scapegoat.[6] What do these mechanisms consist of? They comprise resolving conflicts caused by the antagonistic desires we have for the same objects, by transferring our violence to an innocent victim which we sacrifice in order to have social peace once again. The entire myth of separation is based on the logic of victimisation:

- Ndun, the wise old man, is sacrificed by God to serve as a new foundation for the social group which will take the crocodile as a totem and legitimise its cohesion through its relationship with an illustrious ancestor;

- an old woman and a young girl are sacrificed to create a ritual covenant by which estranged groups would establish peace among themselves;

- animals are sacrificed to seal a 'union', a 'covenant', to set up a new order of life where the blood of animals and that of the human being would combine and thus establish a pact, through which human beings, animals and the whole of nature would be committed to an ecological obligation that would guarantee their future security;

- the Creator sacrifices himself by withdrawing from the world: He dies to the human world in order to return to his universe which, henceforth, is separated from that of human beings.

Confronted by the logic of victimisation whose magnitude in the workings of the human mind R. Girard had already shown, the figure of Christ is offered as a principle deconstructing the place where violence occurs, as the protector of the intellect and of the absolute will to restructure the spirit for the advent of a new order of being and society.

What is being deconstructed? Faith in the victimising mechanism itself. By his own sacrifice, he shows the futility of all sacrifices where blood plays the role of reparation and ransom; he nullifies the plan of submission to a secret and bloodthirsty divinity whose authoritarian precepts and humiliating laws would have been internalised. With the presence of Christ, it is no longer the question of paying a ransom to the divine Moloch, but of making the human heart and the spirit of the people, the real issue of the sacrifice: the fertile place for humane values and the commitment to build a society based on the plan of God.[7]

Christ reveals this plan and establishes it as the source of a universal brotherhood, the real meaning of human culture and the way of salvation whenever social groups are tempted to destroy the fabric of their common belonging to humanity by embroiling themselves in conflicts.

With regard to this brotherhood, he reveals an essential truth: the need for a vision of the relationship where he himself is the mediator in my relationship with my neighbour, with the world and with God. This Christ, who is the universal mediator, does not give himself to us by means of a secret and exclusivist path only known to Christians, but is the vital reality, apart from which humanity is unthinkable.

In him, a humanism of faith, charity and hope takes shape, where Africa would feel called to renew the orientation of its quest for salvation, that is, for fundamental meaning.

- *A humanism of faith*. This concerns the conviction that our common belonging to humanity makes us capable of believing in ourselves, having faith in our ability to act as ourselves and to live as human beings, so as to be able to build a destiny not based on insignificance, inconsistency and the devaluation of our lives, but on human profundity and vital solidarity.

- *A humanism of charity*. This concerns the need to work to make love the creative fabric of social life in the broadest sense of the term;love that is not a vague sentimental space or generous abstraction for romantic emotions, but a spirit that is capable of building solid institutions, rules of community life and space for creativity, where happiness is possible as a manifestation of the Spirit of God.

- *A humanism of hope*. This concerns the commitment to always live in such a way that human life should approximate the plan of God for generations to come, on the understanding that the basic values of humanity have meaning, only if they make of us the builders of an Africa in which there is happiness and living fullness for our children and the generations that will live on our land after we have left the scene.

If we consider faith, charity and hope as the main virtues of our existence, we shall understand that, at the heart of African humanism, centred on respect for differences, unity of life between social groups, vital union of all beings in the power of God, as well as on the autonomy of space for freedom and human responsibility where traditions develop and blood brotherhood is constituted, Christ enriches our quest for a new vision of society. This means the possibility of a new existence that lays the foundations of a 'society of shared humanity', a society where brotherhood blossoms in a common quest for well-being, progress, prosperity and development for all. When this Christ is born again at the heart of our own culture and brings us to new birth in our vocation to incarnate the human in the world - that, then, is the way of salvation.

Footnotes

[1] R. Jaouen has already analysed this myth in his book, *L'eucharistie du Mil* (Paris: Karthala, 1997). L.-V. Thomas and R. Luneau make very interesting analyses in their book, *La terre africaine et ses religions*.

[2] Thomas & Luneau, *La terre africaine*, p.137.

[3] Jan Patocka, *Essais hérétiques sur la philosophie de l'histoire* (Paris: Verdier, 1981).

[4] Blaise Cendrars, *Anthologie nègre* (Paris: Buchet/Chestel, 1947).

[5] We are grateful to our colleague Francis Grob, of the Protestant Higher Institute of Theology, in Ndounge (Cameroon), for drawing our attention to the theodicy problem as a spiritual pathology.

[6] Cf. René Girard, *La violence et le sacré* (Paris: Gallimard, 1973).

[7] Cf. F. Varillon, *Joie de vivre, joie de croire.*

CHAPTER 6

The myth of creation

Elements of the myth

Africa has produced a multitude of cosmogonic narratives and mythical stories about the creation of the world and the destiny of humanity, that are very rich and varied in the meaning that can be given them, both spiritually and theologically.

From myths of the original egg to legends of the creation of everything by the word and breath of the Creator, narratives about God the potter who models human beings in the image of the Demiurge, the player who proceeds by trial and error before attaining perfection, there is a vast range of meaningful dynamics within which a christological study of the African 'grove of initiation' is possible and can be rationally articulated.

In this wide field, it seemed useful to us to take as the point of departure, the myth of creation, which in our opinion, is the most complex and most fruitful with respect to the problem of salvation and the meaning of human existence. We present some of its main points here following the version given by Blaise Cendrars.

At the very beginning of creation, when nothing at all existed, neither heaven nor earth, men, beasts or places, God existed and he was called Nzamé. Nzamé was a three-in-one God and comprised Nzamé, Mébère and Nkwa.

Having created heaven and earth, Nzamé chose heaven for himself, and with his breath populated the earth with all the animals and all the things that inhabit it.

At a council meeting, Nzamé asked Mébère and Nkwa what they thought of his creation, and this is the answer he received. 'We see many animals but we do not see their leader. We see many plants, but we do not see their master.' The three-in-one Nzamé then decided to provide creation with a master who would oversee the earth.

During their first attempt, an elephant was chosen for this task on account of his wisdom, the leopard for his cunning power and the monkey for his mischief and flexibility.

This first attempt, however, proved unsatisfactory. The leader had to be a being that looked 'almost similar' to the three-in-one Nzamé; and this created being was man. The three-in-one Nzamé then invested him with force, power and beauty'; and made him master of all that existed. They said to him: 'Like us, you have life, everything is under your control, you are the master'. This man was called Fam.

But this first man turned out to be a disappointment. Taking advantage of the fact that God was in heaven and that he was the sole master on earth, he 'became proud, and made fun of the Creator'.

In order to punish him, God sent thunder which destroyed everything - beasts, birds and fish. Unfortunately, however, in creating the first man God had told him,'You will not die'. Since God does not take back what he gives, the first man was burnt. I have no idea what became of him; and even though he is alive, I do not not know where, since my ancestors did not tell me that.

Having destroyed the living beautiful system he had created, God began to regret his actions and sought to do something better. The three-in-one Nzamé spread out a new layer of earth, out of which a tree emerged. As the tree grew, one of its seeds which fell to the ground led the the emergence of another tree. Any leaf that fell from the branch subsequently grew until it began to walk; and these turned into animals of all kinds, the elephant, leopard, antelope and tortoise. Similarly, any leaf that fell into water, swam till it became either a fish, a sardine, a mullet, a crab, an oyster, a mussel or a swimming creature of a kind. The earth then became what it was before and what it still is today.

The three-in-one Nzamé then decided at a meeting to create a new man. 'We shall create a man again just like Fam, with the same legs and same arms. This time, however, we shall turn his head and he shall see death'; and thus it was done. That man, my friends, was like you and me. That man was called Sékoumé.

For man not to be alone, the three-in-one Nzamé told man to make himself a woman from a tree. This, Sékoumé did, and he called her

Mbongue. These first beings were made up of two parts: the external one, *Gnoul* which is the body, and the other one, *Nsimim,* which lives in the *Gnoul,* provides the shade and is responsible for the existence of *Gnoul.* When a man dies, it is *Nsimim* which leaves the *Gnoul,* though it does not itself die. The seat of *Nsimim* is the 'eye'.

The first couple had three children: Nkouré (the idiot, the bad one), Békalé (he who does not think of anything) and Mèfère, the third (he who is good and skillful). They also had daughters. According to the narrator, Mèfère, is the father of our community; the others, Nkouré and Békalé are the fathers of other communities.

The first man that God buried in the earth 'dug and dug and one day came out'. He is the one who does all evil to mankind.

God gives human beings laws by which to order their lives and so live happily. He says to them: 'Here are the laws I give you and which you will obey in the future:

You shall no longer steal in your community.
You shall not kill anyone who does not harm you.
You shall not go and eat others at night.
That is all I am asking of you, live in peace in your villages.
Those who will pay heed to my commandments will be rewarded.
I will give them their wages and I will punish the others'.

Those punished by God 'go wandering, suffering and screaming in the night. At the time when darkness fills the earth and people are afraid, they enter into villages, killing or wounding those they see, doing them all the evil they can'. Dances and sacrifices that people offer to them have no effect on their power to do evil.

And when all they know are dead, it is only then that they hear Ngôfiô Ngôfiô, the bird of death. They suddenly become lean, very lean, and then they die! Where do they go, my children? You know as well as I do. A long time ago, before crossing the river, they stayed on a big flat stone, where they used to suffer from cold, terrible cold (...). And when all of them have gone through the curse, Nzamé imprisons them in Ototolane, the terrible place of great misery, for a very, very long time....

As for the good people, they return to their villages after their death. They live happily among people, funeral celebrations characterised by mourning and dances make them joyful. At night, they draw closer to those they knew and loved, place before their eyes pleasant dreams and tell them what to do in order to live longer, acquire great wealth, have faithful wives, many children and kill many animals during hunting expeditions.

> And when all they know are dead, it is only then that they hear Ngôfiô Ngôfiô, the bird of death. They then become extremely fat and die! My children, where do they go after their death? You know as I do, that God takes them up and places them with him in the evening star. From there, they look at us, they see us and are happy when we celebrate their memory by dancing. It is the eyes of all those that are dead that make the star so bright.

Such is the cosmogonic myth. Those of us with a Christian perspective have surely discovered in this myth elements of the Christian vision of the world. While the 'three-in-one-Nzamé' brings to our mind the idea of the Trinity, the notion of breath reminds us of God's creative breath and that of the Spirit, and the idea of reward and punishment reminds us of heaven and hell in the Christian tradition.

Nsimim and *Gnoul* have something to do with the classical notions of the soul and body, which have been naively incorporated into a certain tradition of Christianity. Let us, however, be careful of these deceitful similarities. The myth of creation recounted here is in keeping with its own anthropological, theological and eschatological framework, as opposed to Christian anthropology, theology and eschatology.

The main problem it tackles is that of human destiny and the meaning of life, from the perspective of what is really worth living if we want to become real human beings. At the heart of this destiny, there is the relationship which humankind has with a reality which we must not lose sight of, namely anthropological catastrophe represented by the split between the first and second creation, between Fam, the first man, and mankind after the man's punishment, placed under the authority of a new man, Sékoumé. This catastrophe is, in fact, Fam himself in his evil action at the heart of the world.

It can be said that it is the problem of the externalisation of evil, of its permanent link with humanity which cannot assert itself as human, without realising that a certain spirit of suffering and destruction clings to human beings at all times. Whereas one would have expected that the myth should come up with victories in the fight against Fam, this myth, on the contrary, develops as if his presence in the world was not a major problem, as if there was no ontological relationship between the pride which destroyed the first man and the very destiny of the new humanity. Fam has nothing in common with Adam. His mistake does not affect humanity in an originally ontological manner. The problem of salvation and the meaning of life does not depend on him or on his guilt. We do not live in the ancient world characterised by the seal of some original sin. It is a completely new world; the place of a new relationship with God represented by the law as the way to happiness; and is thus better than the first world.

The difference between the new world and the old is distinct. Whereas the first world was the outcome of One Person's initiative, without the visible involvement of the plural nature of the Creator (the three-in-one Nzamé), the second creation is the result of concerted action and divine deliberation, the result of a plurality which asserts itself as the place of collegial intelligence where unity is the real creative wisdom. As a product of this wisdom, the new world and the new man assume their responsibility in the law which is the human translation of creative wisdom.

This law which is absent in the first creation, builds a relationship in which the right to life, prosperity and security constitute the backbone of communal existence. Like creation, the law given by God to humankind is not the initiative of one of the three who comprise Nzamé, but a decision taken by the three of them together in a meeting. This deliberative consensus affects all rules which make up human life as structured by the Creator, that is, according to the canons of a plurality bound to form an ethical unity. Right at the beginning of this new world which includes the new man, plurality, deliberation and consensus constitute the basis of society.

It should be pointed out that this new world does not belong to man alone; it is a world in which the woman will have her place as 'the other part of man', the person through whom the world obtains basic balance according to the perspectives which God opens. The fact that the woman originates from the tree does not mean that she is of a different species or is inferior to man, as a certain patriarchal interpretation of the myth would make us think. Rather, if we link the symbol of the tree to the creative word which is represented by the order given to man to make himself his real living essence by the creation of a woman, we realise that a real theology of compatibility between the masculine and the feminine takes root here. The figure of the woman appears mainly as the figure of the link between man and his true essence, between man-woman and the world, the way by which the tree (symbol of the whole ecosystem), becomes integrated in the human order as a component of this order. At the same time, by the same ontological constitution woman shares with man, she is a backbone that is just as important to social life as man himself. Just as the three-in-one Nzamé consists of only one person in the work of creating and organising the universe and humankind, man and woman constitute one person in two, and have by their unity, found a vital reality where the entire creation acquires a human and divine meaning. This means the institution of the cultural link as a powerful reality: a link between the Creator and the creatures, a link between the natural world and human world, a link between the masculine and the feminine, a link between humanity and divinity.

The whole myth is based on this ontological conception of the link which alone gives us a deep knowledge of God's intention when he created the woman from the ecological order, of which the tree, in its relation with the world of humankind, is the figure. This intention is clear. All social life is based on the ontological cultural link. Alongside plurality, deliberation and consensus, this cultural link is the basis of the African vision of the world as the myth helps us to understand.

It is not only a problem of a vital link between divinity, humanity and the totality of beings according to a vital principle on which an ecology for the promotion of life is built in Africa, but also of the link between the order of basic values represented by the ancestors, the order of the social life we live here and now, and the order of requirements which are necessary for humankind, so that future generations live in a world where they are assured of happiness or of the possibility of attaining that happiness.

It is significant that the myth in itself constantly reminds us that it is the word of our fathers, and our fathers thus have a first hand meaning of it, in which the narrator participates in order to give meaning to the present and open prospects for the future. It is here that the problem of salvation acquires its full meaning as a quest for roots, for foundations. If the myth focuses on the creation and origin of the world, it is mainly in order to give to human beings the keys to guide them in this world. This myth is a kind of set of instructions for life, based on the directions given by the ancestors, for all future generations.

Christ and the ethic of creation

Once the meaning of the myth is clear, it is useful to consider it as the meeting point where Africa welcomes Jesus Christ and begins to dialogue with him, in 'the grove of initiation'.[1] When Christ penetrates this grove and joins the discussion on the problem of salvation as a quest for the origin of humanity, what meaning does he give to African research on how to interpret human destiny?

As in the two previous myths, it is necessary to view Christ from two angles. The first is what we have referred to as the illuminating and revitalising interiority, that is, the character of Jesus of Nazareth as a figure that is internal to our history and culture, and on which new light is shed by God. At this level, Christ brings to light the human limits of meaning as the myth of creation sees it.

We think, first, of the attempt at a perverse totalisation which makes us forget that our African spiritual history is not limited to the explicit and foundational word of our ancestors, but extends to what Christ himself, as 'one of our own', prescribes as the meaning of life. This means that the revelation of God the Creator as the 'three-in-one Nzamé' should be interpreted in the light of the holy Trinity: God 'who is pure love', to use once again Father F. Varillon's expression. If God 'is pure love', the dimensions of plural unity, constructive deliberation and creative consensus which the African myth reveals, become the constituent component of love not only as divine energy, but as a social relationship which transforms the entire human order.

We must emphasise this point, because in the myth, the social values which the 'three-in-one Nzamé' promote in the creation of man, are those of wisdom, power, force, cunning and beauty, rather than that of love as such. Yet for everything to change at the very heart of the foundation of a culture, it suffices that all these qualities be understood as intrinsic to love. If wisdom is the wisdom of love, if power is the power of love, and if it were so for cunning and beauty, the type of culture and civilisation we would propose to build, would obviously be different from the one which governs our societies today.

This consideration leads us to another problem which the myth poses. In naming the children of the first couple, the myth suggests that only the community of those who narrate this myth are descendants of the good son, while other communities originate either from Nkouré (the idiot or bad one), or from Békalé (he who does not think of anything). We are taken back to the problem of ethnocentric separation which had already been brought up by the previous myth. Here the perspective is deeper and more enlightening. We are at the very foundation of ethnocentrism and ethnic conflicts. These are not imported and invented by strangers to divide us Africans, but are somehow part of our essential nature in our myths of origins. Thus, the ethnic problem is woven into the fabric of our myths and our cosmogonic narratives, as we have recounted them through the centuries.

We should conduct a thorough analysis of mythological narratives, tales and legends which have shaped the minds of children in the educational process, to see whether evil is not found in the heart of our culture itself. In the dialogue which we establish with him in the heart of our grove, Christ shows us precisely that the problem lies in the nature of our own world. He does this by opening another horizon, namely that of narratives which should create a responsible brotherhood. They include:

- the narrative of creation as the work of God 'who is pure love' - the power of the trinitarian life;
- the narrative of the love of God, a God who goes all the way to

accept the death of his son on the cross;

- the narrative of love as the permanent presence of God in his creation and in the depths of humanity, by the power of the Paraclete, a regenerative and vigorous renewing presence.

The ethic that these narratives establish is far-reaching and embraces relationships between man and woman. In the myth of creation, the temptation to make a patriarchal interpretation which makes the woman inferior, is ever present. With the presence of Christ, this temptation completely disappears. There is no possibility of viewing the relationship between man and woman from the point of view of domination, oppression or exploitation. It is not a relationship based on force, but one of compatibility based on God's original plan. The anthropological fertility of the woman revealed in Christ, constitutes an authentic way of life and respect for humanity. Beginning with Christ, the myth of creation is devoid of its patriarchal potential and takes on potentialities of mutual enrichment between man and woman. A new image of humanity emerges to strengthen Africa, as it plays an invaluable part in enhancing the role of the woman in relation to the universe, in relation to the invisible, and in relation to the world of the ancestors. Where the myth tends to forget this wealth of the African way of life, Christ recalls it and recreates it as a social way of salvation, a love pact.

But Christ does not only reveal to Africa these internal truths. He also reveals himself as the absolute otherness - another perspective from which God speaks to us and sows deep within us a new word of life.

This word is that of the principle of the new heaven and the new earth which is the basis of humanity in Africa, and which cannot be reduced to social wisdom and the art of living. It is the 'foolishness' of God revealed in the strong determination to model the world on all the values which Christ represents and on the absolute horizon he opens.

Here it is a question of knowing that in Christ something new is beginning. For he did not come only to fulfil the word of the ancestors and strengthen us in the vision of the world they bequeathed to us, but to fulfil a new vision of what it means to be human: the logic of God's reign which is pure love.

This logic involves placing the totality of human existence under God's authority - his being, his word and the meaning which he opens up to our existence. The God this logic reveals is the very God of Jesus Christ, God as can only be discovered in Jesus Christ - fullness and superabundance of love.

From the revelation of this radical theological truth, a double requirement follows. There is the urgent need to create and to set up within society communities of love, vibrant channels of love in action, by which social life can be transformed into a solid fabric according to absolute love that is God himself, as the principle of the incarnation of love in the human being and in the community. The link that could develop here is not the simple link of blood or belonging to the same geographical area, but links in the Spirit of God manifested and embodied in Jesus Christ. He thus becomes the lamp by which we perceive the ultimate meaning of a social relationship: love as vital energy and fullness of happiness.

There is the urgent need also for a vital link between all communities of love whose life would be the reality of the Church: this universal dynamic of those who identify themselves with Jesus Christ as the fertile soil of the new world and creator of the future. Here, we are beyond all petty ethnocentric or religious and denominational perspectives. We are in God as a principle of universal love in action, the Church as a living sphere of true humanity, real solidarity and brotherly responsibility, so that no human person nor society should be excluded from love as the fullness of happiness.

The absolute distinctiveness of Jesus Christ thus changes the meaning of relationships between Africa and those who introduced Christianity with an ambiguous Christ, so linked to the universe of others that he risked reducing himself to a geographical exteriority which Africans 'could not absorb'.

Considered as the wholly other place of the revelation of God as 'He who only is love', Christ places Africans and their evangelisers under the same universal human obligation: that of building a world based on solidarity whose foundational myths would not be limited to their respective cultures, but be deeply transformed by being plunged once more into the Spirit of God the Father and Creator, God of love, with the intention of making all of humankind the sphere of his love and shared happiness.

God entrusts this mission of his to communities of love which make up the Church. He makes it the meaning of our destiny and the stake of our salvation, here and now. Such is the way to salvation.

Footnotes

[1] A perspective found in Efoé Julien Penoukou's important article published in *Chemins de la christologie africaine*, under the title: 'Christologie au village', 69-106. An anthropological analysis based on data from a myth of origin of the Ewe-Mina people (in Benin and Togo) has led the author to a perception of Christ that is deeply African and genuinely Christian. The same approach guides us throughout our study of African myths as the core of the 'grove of initiation'. An English version of the article is found in Robert Schreiter (ed.), *Faces of Jesus in Africa* (London: SCM Press, 1991).

CHAPTER 7

Christology and the ultimate destiny of humanity

In-depth approach

The interpretation we have just given to the analysis of the three creation myths, and the integration of Christ into their scope of significance, as tested in the light of Egyptology and the study of African traditions, have not yet exhausted the problem of salvation, since it should be examined also from a theological perspective.

They can be considered as a preliminary approach which makes it possible to gradually dig deeper. Because deep down, the problem of salvation is that of the ultimate relationship between life and death, between good and evil, between the forces of light and the powers of darkness, it is a problem of destiny, as Engelbert Mveng would have said. This concept of salvation is really

> the crux of the basic problem of culture, civilisation, and human destiny. It poses the problem of the meaning of life and history, and demonstrates that human history must obey precise laws which are those of the quest for the victory of life over death.[1]

The three myths that we have analysed have something very significant to teach us on this issue, from a christological point of view; something we have only touched upon and whose essential meaning we would now like to bring to light.

The myth of Isis and Osiris presents us with a tragedy, at the end of which death appears to be a strange, enriching immobility at the centre of life. Death is there in the form of a cold solidity, a silent rigid force by which every reality is defined. One understands why the inhabitants of ancient Egypt spent so much time dealing with its reality, getting themselves constantly ready for it, in order to master all the rites that could help them find their way in the other world, and to master the mysteries of the world beyond. As the very centre of life, it fascinates, hypnotises, at the same time as it controls behaviour and opens up a horizon of meaning.

The ancient Egyptian Book of the Dead is interesting from that perspective. It shows permanent traffic between the living and the dead, in the hope of an ultimate liberation, which may constitute either a happy entry into the world beyond, or a plunging into the rigid and cold immobility of the here below, symbolised by mummies that lie silent for centuries inside their sarcophaguses.

The significance of the solution which the myth of Isis and Osiris gives to the problem of salvation, is interesting. According to this creation myth:

- the living can give the dead creative meaning by being connected to them through their inventive power, by drawing from them the power of imagination, which is available as a way of living and being;

- the dead are the harbingers of life and the reservoir of vital power where the origins of culture are found;

- for the living, the dead do not have a meaning that belongs only to the world beyond, but a rich presence in which every person directs his intentions towards the final resting place for all beings.

But the most important thing in this vision of the dead, is that it places the individual on a long road to life, which he must tread to attain his 'glorious body', in order to play his part in a cosmic responsibility which places humankind above the gods, so to speak.

What is at stake in this quest, as the Egyptologist, Georges Kolpaktchy, points out, is 'the issue of integral humanism' - humanity becomes the centre of the universe.

> The deceased is (...) conscious of his cosmic nature: that his physical body, his soul, his spirit, his 'other self' (...) and his 'glorious body' among other things are the effects of a long evolution extending over billions of years. Furthermore, in some respects, the perfect and sanctified man would be superior to the gods: he would be their saviour and their redeemer (...). He would deliver them from evil, be their hope, the guarantor of their future, their successor and their ideal'.[2]

The link between the living and the dead is thus an essential ethical ideal. It is the link to Osiris's spirit in order to accomplish the ideal of the *Maat*, that unified concept of truth, righteousness and justice which maintains the balance of the world and the ontological substance of beings.

The Egyptologist, Bilolo Mubabinge, from the Democratic Republic of Congo, appreciates this problem. He sees in the cosmo-theologies of ancient Egypt, vast frescos for indicating the meaning of being and of humanity's final destiny - to become an ideal, even for the gods.[3]

Going further than Bilolo Mubabinge and Georges Kolpaktchy, the Cameroonian historian, Kange Ewane, puts the problems in their right perspective. According to him, the heart of the metaphysics of ancient Egypt is the inclusion of humankind, and reality as a whole, in divine power.[4] It was not only the ethical problem of the relationship between life and death that was at stake, there was also the very transformation of the order of human life: meaning as ontogenesis, a revolution in the structure of reality, where only positive forces would be released through enormous concentric circles of life linked together by the rich vibrations of an ecological order.

In the 'myth of separation', the wise old Ndun plays the role, more or less, of Osiris.

Ndun is death as foundation, death as enrichment. He is the foundation upon which God builds the new order: the order of responsible brotherhood, of human autonomy and freedom after the death of theodicy.

Thanks to him, the Creator unites life and death in a single scope of meaning, in a single and unique social stability where rites give meaning to life and life acquires a significance worthy of humanity.

It should be recalled here that everything in the myth centres around death in the form of a sacrifice:

- Ndun's death and its sacrificial character is obvious even though it is not called a sacrifice;
- the death of the two women sacrificed to pacify the society;
- the death of many animals which constitutes a pledge of a racial covenant and even of a covenant of humanity as a species;
- the death of trees and plants, symbol of the covenant of life;
- the death of the Creator himself who decides to go away from men and give them free space for their fulfilment and their development.

These accumulated deaths constitute the basis of brotherhood, freedom and responsibility of humanity and society, the death of theodicy as a spiritual concept of reality.

The objective of the myth is clear; it is in relation to death that the meaning of existence and of salvation as the ultimate for the fulfilment of being, takes shape.

We should allow ourselves to be enriched by the vital power of the dead, that is, the power of images, values, representations and hopes which constitute, in a culture, the spiritual journey of the community in the course of its history. He who has not established this relationship with his deceased ancestors cannot really have access to the human. He who has not really established this link with these strange stone tombs that the myth depicts as solid symbols of the way to the invisible, lacks vital substance. Death is in life as the very path of sacrifice, the way by which we integrate within ourselves the Spirit of the race: that power, which makes us responsible for the generations that will follow us on earth.

It can be said that the race we are talking about refers to all the communities that must co-exist after a just and equitable sharing of vital space. Such sharing is not possible without an experience of death, that is, of sacrifice. Sacrifice is the symbol of death in life. That is why it is the way to salvation.

We now understand why the problem of the relationship between life and death does not depend only on the order of social organisation as revealed in the myth of Isis and Osiris, nor does it depend exclusively on a fundamental anthropological order revealed in the legend of the separation and the withdrawal of God, but rather and above all, it depends on the very order of creation. It acquires an initiatory dimension, on the basis of which are built the foundational values of the human.

The myth of creation which embraces to a large extent the two preceding myths, is the fundamental place where, by the manifestation of death as the initiatory enrichment of life, it has been clearly shown that every person and every society must internalise the meaning of death in an initiatory manner, and thus situate their own journey in the meaning of true life.

Salvation here is not merely a personal matter, but also communal. We can also state it the other way round and say that salvation is not merely a communal problem, but a personal one. This double emphasis on the perspective of death as the initiatory principle of both individual and communal enrichment of life, shows to what extent physical and natural death, instead of being a catastrophe, is part of the very order of life. Death has been included in the divine plan and is definitely part of the new creation, so that humanity would avoid the excess and arrogance of deifying itself or deifying some individuals whom it would idolise.

The problem, for humanity, is not to mix up the order of death with that of evil, nor is it, more precisely, to make evil a principle that sows death. He who practises evil will suffer eternal damnation; he will be thrown into *ototolane*.

On the other hand, it is goodness as a principle that gives meaning to death. He who devotes himself to being good, will be rewarded with happiness, the evening star, after having enriched life with all the powers of fullness.

That is why, before they disappear for good, the dead still stay on in the villages to bestow kindness and blessings, or misfortune and catastrophe.

Christ, Love and Death

If we consider that the three myths analysed constitute the sphere of meaning which enables Africa to enter into dialogue with Christ, then the foundations of a christology of salvation become clearer. It is through his relationship with death that the personality of Christ renews, enriches and revitalises the African mythological space in which he is integrated.

Christ in his death reveals God who shows himself to be pure love in his passion for humanity, whom he created in his image and to whom he reveals the way to fulfilment: love as the heart of life, 'the sacrifice of self as an expression of love', to quote Father Varillon.

By the power of the good news shared in the community, Jesus's message opens a horizon not only of investment in the world beyond, but of a new destiny for humanity.

By ensuring a dialogue between Christ and the mythological foundations of African societies, we welcome Christ as one of our own. 'Our brother-become-God and God-become-our-brother', according to the beautiful confession of faith of a child from Kinshasa during a catechism class.

This brother-become-God takes on all our experience of death by including it in the plan of the new heaven and the new earth, the horizon of death transformed into a glorious community of love that gathers people of all races, languages, peoples, nations, cultures and civilisations, in the city where God himself lives and illumines everything.

By taking Christ first as a figure internal to our own culture, we understand that his whole destiny is to show the fruitfulness of death when it is assumed from the perspective of life for others, for the community, society and humanity. Without exaggerating its value in opening up perspectives to the world beyond, nor reducing it to a non-event, Christ takes death not as the subject of a philosophical discourse, but as a terrible reality that could be absurd if the world was shut in on itself, without any thought of an ultimate relationship with God. According to him, there is the need to give meaning to death by seeing it as a gift of oneself to the living. It is in the link with life that death can become a true blessing.

Jesus avoids giving the impression that he knows a great deal about what happens after a person's last breath. He only gives indications that call for each person's responsibility in the face of God's judgement as well as the need for each person not to be deaf to the distress of those who lose a member of their family and who need God's consolation and that of their fellow human beings. To him, the enigma and mystery of death constitute a trial for the spirit.

Confronted with his own death, he did not have the splendid serenity of Socrates or the quiet certainty of those who know that 'the dead are not dead'. He was gripped by fear, he perspired blood and water before he could submit himself to the will of his Father, as the only one who gives meaning to death for the living by opening the great horizon of resurrection as a new life.

That is why the cross on which Christ was nailed reveals him to us not only as 'our brother-become-God', or as one of us going back to the ancestors and enriching our village with his kindness, but as quite a different person coming from a different place of significance and going to a world which he alone can open to us - the Father's world. He is God coming to us to give us a new birth in his love and to accomplish in us a new destiny; and we ourselves going to God in our quest for total renewal.

From this perspective, Jesus confronted all the negativities in our existence and assumed the terrible and terrifying aspect of the human condition. On the cross, in the flesh and spirit of a man condemned to death and subjected to terrible torture, Jesus experienced powerful forces of evil coming together to fight humankind: the unfathomable depths of suffering and the darkness of a hopeless death. Death and suffering reveal the tragic nature of life and block the doors of hope. Jesus was confronted with the storms of the absurd, the tempests of the annihilation of all his physical powers and all the faith his disciples had placed in him as the Messiah.

But he also knew that on the cross, God was truly revealing himself as he is. He knew that the meaning and significance of the destiny of the Son of Man was revealed there; there and nowhere else.

What is revealed in this very place? An essential truth which E. J. Penoukou aptly describes thus:

> In the event of Jesus Christ is inscribed (...) the radical faithfulness of God's love for humanity and for the whole creation. It indicates the extent to which creation has always been called to find its fulfilment in Christ (cf. Rom. 8, 12), how far the finality of Christ's solidarity is to achieve fulfilment for humankind, to satisfy his aspirations to be more human.

> By experiencing in his human life the anguish and the hopes of men and women, by accepting to die in order to overcome death and by rising from the dead to fullness of life, Jesus Christ passes through the sequence of life/death/life as the way to accomplish salvation for humankind. In other words, Jesus integrates into himself human life, dies a human death, and enters a transformed life, not for himself, but for humanity. He thus penetrates the

mystery of the human in a unique and absolutely distinctive way, and as Pope John-Paul II puts it, he invests the profundity of the human being with his divine being'.[5]

This is the same truth about Jesus Christ which Father F. Varillon described in language even more striking, profound and realistic. According to him:

Love is stronger than death, on condition that it should first be stronger than life. Love is stronger than life, it is sacrifice and it is death. Love is stronger than death, it is resurrection. In other words, sacrifice, which is partial death, and death, which is a complete sacrifice, transform the life of flesh and blood into life according to the spirit.[6]

That is the main point and the true re-creation of humanity, which he achieves. To move from life according to the dictates of flesh and blood, to life according to the spirit, is to make a personal, communal, social, and cultural conversion, which is the basis of a new world. Henceforth, this conversion is the lever of the salvation of humankind, the seed of love as sacrifice and resurrection, as a plan for another quality of life, life in Jesus Christ.

The idea of resurrection as new life is important here. It is a matter of God's initiative, as he wants to give people a vital new reality, to open up to them the fullness of the manifestation of himself in the heavenly Jerusalem, where there is no temple, no synagogue, no mosque and no grove of initiation, but the pure and total presence of God for his people.

This salvation through resurrection is the true fruitfulness of Christ's death. It shows that in going back to his Father, Jesus transmitted to the world the spirit of the reversal of values which is the foundation of a new way of being, of living, of thinking and of acting; not self-enrichment, but the strength to work for the enrichment of others; not domination, but solidarity and brotherly responsibility; not confidence in human beings and in their ability to save themselves, but faith in God who makes available for all humanity his free and saving love.

Believing in God's salvation means, therefore, in the words of E. Dussel, choosing the path of the transformation of minds and social structures as required by the Spirit of God in Christ's revealed will for humanity, which involves fighting against negative forces which bring hardship to human beings.

The Father, the Son and the Spirit thus lay the foundations of a culture and a civilisation of commitment to love, which is the only true path for human existence and God's light on the destiny of peoples, the fulfilment of 'the grove of initiation' in the 'splendid courtyard of the Lord God'.

Footnotes

[1] E. Mveng, *Théologie, libération et cultures africaines*, 132.

[2] G. Kolpaktchy, *Introduction au livre des morts des anciens Egyptiens* (Paris: Stock, 1993), 23.

[3] Cf. Bilolo Mubabinge, *Les cosmo-théologies philosophiques ou Heliopolis et Hermopolis. Essai de thématisation et de systematisation* (Kinshasa-Libreville-Munich: Publications Universitaires Africaines, 1988).

[4] Cf. Kange Ewane, 'Religions africaines et ecologie', in *Ethique écologique et construction de l'Afrique* (Yaounde-Bafoussam: Clé/SIPCRE, 1997), 119-28.

[5] E. J. Penoukou, 'Christologie au village', in *Chemins de la christologie africaine*, 104.

[6] F. Varillon, *Joie de vivre, joie de croire*.

CHAPTER 8

The courage to be human

In the 'grove of initiation' where our ancestors recognise him as the symbol of the depth of our creativity and our power of life from time immemorial, Jesus Christ, who is both internal light, enriching exteriority, and radical otherness, is given a peculiar status at the heart of African culture: the status of a living force who places Africans on the path to courage, the main characteristics of which can be defined clearly.

First of all, it is the courage of the 'complete story' about ourselves, the honest view of our existence, our history and our reality in its high and low points, its sad and happy moments. Thanks to Christ, we can look at ourselves as we are in the founding myths of our destiny, to discover that we are neither angels nor demons, but human beings in search of the meaning of our existence, building our society by promoting the positive values of life, and by fighting against the negative values of death that are permanently interwoven with them. Beings such as we are, always trying to build for ourselves a meaning that denies the dark realities of our lives and exalts the legend of our ancient greatness, always prone to build for ourselves a glorious destiny by erasing our cultural pathologies, we needed someone to come and explain our condition to us very clearly. That person who had to come, is Christ, the son of our womb and the son of God's womb, whose way of salvation is to make us true to the Creator, true to other civilisations and true to ourselves. Christ is salvation through the truth.[1]

Beside the courage of 'the complete story' about ourselves, is the courage of radical conversion to newness, when it sets us free and fulfils us. Jesus Christ embodies a new word, a new destiny in a visible human body, which is revealed as the measure of God on earth as well as the measure of humankind in God's plan, as the only one who, as Father Jean Cardonel puts it, proclaims God', as much as he proclaims humanity.

Given the ancient word of our fathers, this new reality requires a new word, a new form of spiritual life and a new understanding of the relationship between God and humankind.

An old African traditional priest from Tokombere in the northern part of Cameroon understood this truth very well. Having realised that the impact of the gospel of Jesus Christ, which spread all over his village, was so great that it could not be ignored in the education of the new generation of Africans, he called the priest of the Catholic mission and told him the truth in words of great wisdom: 'I know that one day or the other, your 'sacrifice' will replace mine, the word of Jesus Christ will replace my ancestral and ancient word without destroying it. I am going to die a happy man because I know there will always be a sacrifice made in our village. That is very important. I hand over to you. Continue with what our ancestors started, and of which I was the high priest.'

Father Grégoire Cadoche, a French missionary in Tokombere, who recounted this dialogue during a training session in Batié (Cameroon) in 1997, drew a lesson of great spiritual significance from it. What is at stake in Jesus Christ, he thinks, is the conversion of Africa to a new word of life which requires a new sacrifice, the eucharist, as a sharing of Jesus Christ among people, a sharing of his spirit, incarnation and of his plan in a society which needs to become a society of love, like God himself who is love. Let us call this new reality the eucharistic society.

A new spirit must be born, but it must not destroy the deeply human element in the word of our ancestors. Rather, it must carry it forward, assume it, fulfil it, and so raise the human to a higher level, meeting the need for humanity to be at the very level of God, at the level of love. Since he who reveals this word is truly the son of our culture as well as the wholly-other coming from the presence of God, he establishes both a new line of participation and a break from the old allegiances, by means of which our original myths may be reassessed and reconsidered.

Henceforth, in Christ, Africa's spiritual life becomes essentially a eucharistic reality, a happiness shared according to the spirit of Jesus Christ, who is the true son of our ancestors, and true son of God.

Thanks to this double status, he is able to save us from the danger of letting our past and our history become sterile monuments, a mere legend that we recount so as to conceal from ourselves our own present weakness and our cultural defects. He saves us from our tendency to turn to the world of our forefathers as a way of escaping from the realities of our own world and from the requirements of the future.

In Christ, we are converted to the present and to the future which we have to build, in a spirit that calls up all the creative powers of our fathers in order to incarnate them in God's own creative power, as the dynamic for eucharistic culture and civilisation, and offered to all cultures and civilisations in the world as an essential plan of life and action.

Christ's mediation can and must play this role today; for it is the place for a creative link to a history which it has already transformed into a real place of salvation: the destiny of Israel.

This mediation is also the place for a historical cultural incarnation which can enlighten our understanding of the hermeneutics of our own destiny, the history of the West.

Just as the elect became aware of God and of themselves as basically transformed by a paradoxical Messiah who did not abolish the past, but rather fulfilled it, so also, Africa discovers in Jesus of Nazareth a paradoxical Messiah who opens a new destiny, and demands that Africa should not, as Gabriel Vahanian would say, be politically, economically, culturally, morally and spiritually glued to demonetised ancestral wealth, to a past of dreamlike glorification of the identifying instincts of flesh and blood, but be transformed by God's spirit as part of his purpose for fullness of life for all of humankind.

In the western world, the message of the gospel deconstructed the former pagan world of the Greco-Roman gods, in order to engage an entire civilisation in a radical transformation of its thought patterns and its criteria for action, without, however, invalidating the philosophical and scientific protocols which used to provide the framework for the founding myths of the West. In the same way, the dynamism of Christ should enable Africa to rid herself of the obstacles of her metaphysical weaknesses without rejecting the basic protocols of her founding myths of humanity.

Just as the paradoxical Messiah ceases to be Jewish property but becomes the agent of universal salvation, so Christ becomes for Africa the way of universal salvation through the overall transformation of life and the basic conformity to God's plan. A transformation which is conformity to God and, by this very fact, leads to a new view of the meaning of the whole history of the continent and the entire destiny of our fathers.

Since the Messiah was made part of the culture of the Greco-Roman society where Christianity became a sort of social weapon in a polemical and universalist vision of the world, there is the need to think about an inculturation of the Christian faith into African humanism, with the goal of building a new world based on brotherhood and solidarity.

Christ would constitute not only the leaven for the transformation of our cultural void, but also the critique by which we obtain a clear view of the whole history of Christianity, with its triumphs and its vicissitudes.

It can even be said that henceforth he is the yardstick by which we perceive our ancestors in their view of humanity, while at the same time, they constitute the prism through which we welcome Christ into our own realities. In the same vein, we find in him the measure of humanity against which we measure all human cultures in their claim to build a society of 'shared happiness', to quote Félix Tchotche Mel.

What matters, in fact, is to create, in Christ and by his Spirit, a universal dynamism which makes our ancestors and all the ancestors of humanity, the springboard of a spiritual plan oriented towards the future: a universal civilisation of shared happiness. African humanism revealed by the three myths analysed above, would greatly contribute to the development of that civilisation.

Not only would Africa serve as a spiritual reservoir for Africans, but it would also constitute a rich treasure for all of humankind. Africa would become universalised in Jesus Christ as a continent of the future, for the creation of a fraternal and interdependent world: the continent for the globalisation of love and the human element.

That is why Africa is called upon to acquire from its faith in the Messiah of Nazareth, the courage of serious involvement, in order to build a new society completely free from the forces of decay and disorder that render the future problematic and weaken our creative powers.

This courage means being worthy of our great ancestors whose spirit nourishes all humanity. This is especially so where our African ancestors are concerned, whose spirit should be incarnated in us, the spirit with which they built pyramids, prosperous societies, famous kingdoms and developed a way of living, whose great values of solidarity, hospitality, brotherhood, respect for human beings and promotion of life are enshrined in history. Nonetheless, we cannot consider these Africans as if Christ did not emerge from within our human trajectory and as if he did not come to give a new breath of creative power to our destiny: the power of the Spirit of the God of love, of God who is pure love.

Recapturing the creative spirit which characterises our civilisations by transforming it through the spirit of Jesus Christ, means reorienting all our political, economic, social, cultural, moral and spiritual commitments towards the demands of building a civilisation worthy of our ancestors, all the ancestors of the peoples under the watchful eyes of the God of Jesus Christ. This perspective on salvation is certain to be relevant and enriching for the future.

The courage of the 'complete story', the courage of global conversion, of integral transformation and of commitment in the building of a new society, all this is, in fact, the courage to be human.

It is this courage to be profoundly and completely human which gives to a person and to a society their true substance and which makes them free from the pathologies of insignificance, inconsistency and devaluation of life in an existence devoid of meaning.

For the Africa of today, this courage is revealed in Jesus Christ, this son-of-our-ancestors-become-God, and this God-become-the-son-of-our-ancestors, in the grove of the initiation of our being and our culture. Such is our profession of faith, now and for the future. It is the way of our salvation.

Footnotes

[1] It was the Rev Barthélémy Adoukonou, a theologian from Benin, who made me aware of the Bible as demonstrating this courage of the complete story and helped me conceptualise this courage in the hermeneutics of the overall knowledge Africa must have of herself, of her history and culture.

CHAPTER 9

Christ in his mythological foundations

We have introduced the African 'grove of initiation' and shown how very significant it is for Africa today, confronted by the disorders of lack of self-worth, inconsistency and self-devaluation. We have seen how in this grove, Christ reveals himself at the very heart of African creative power: as an internal illuminator, a re-creative otherness and an external motivator.

We will now tackle another side of the problem: that of the foundational myths through which Jesus of Nazareth gives himself as the meaning in all the areas of significance that we have conferred on him.

If we consider these foundational myths as permanent forces that structure the consciousness that God wants to give to humanity, we shall understand that these forces provide answers to the main questions which the masters of our 'grove of initiation' asked Christ, about his very being, and about the horizon that he opens to us in Africa through salvation.

The 'myth' of the Saviour incarnate

The first myth is the one that defines God's action in the world from the perspective of the universal salvation of humanity. Through the various biblical texts which reveal this myth and the accounts which, from generation to generation, have been narrated in Christian communities, the myth can be presented as follows:

In the beginning, God created the world by his word. Having mastered and organised the original chaos by the breath of his word, he brought all beings to life. He then created man and placed him at the centre of creation as the place of happiness. 'He created man and woman' and entrusted to them the responsibility of cultivating and nurturing the vast and beautiful garden of the world and of making it the place where they would blossom and flourish.

Instead of following the creative word in the guidelines he gave them for total communion with God, the first couple allowed themselves to be seduced by the word of the tempter, the prince of lies and suspicion. At his instigation, they ate the forbidden fruit and brought God's anger and punishment upon themselves. God cursed them and chased them out of the garden. He gave them up to a new way of life characterised by suffering, evil and death. Cut off from the presence of God, and from constant communion with God, their destiny became the story of the loss of original human authenticity: the story of a fall.

In his deep love for his created beings, God did not abandon human beings to their terrible fate and to their errant ways, He sent his Son to come and open for humanity, the way for a new communion with him, the way of salvation. Through his exemplary life, teachings and miracles, the Son opened for humankind the way to a new communion with God. He carried through to the very end the logic of God's love for humanity by dying on the cross, being made a victim of human evil with its countless effects. Arrested, humiliated, tortured and crucified by human beings, his life on earth ended in dreadful failure.

But God brought him back to life on the third day. He made Christ's apparent failure the very instrument of salvation: the radical way of love set before every person 'coming into this world'. That way involves the opening up of humanity to God's Spirit, to the Paraclete responsible for ensuring the presence of the Creator in his creation.

Having ascended into heaven where 'he sits at the right hand of the Father', Christ continues to work by the Spirit through the community of believers who preach his Word, who aim at transforming the world by his Spirit, and who guide human destiny towards the 'summing-up of everything in God', in the new heavens and new earth placed entirely in the light of everlasting happiness.

From the hypothesis that, after listening to the foundational myths of Africa's destiny in 'the grove of initiation', Christ also recounts to Africa this new myth as the founding narrative of his own destiny, we can define the way of salvation in three ways, according to which Africa has to shape its encounter with Christ in the context of salvation.

The vital function of God the Creator

The first aspect is the vital function of God the Creator and its meaning for humanity. Having already talked about the revelation of God as Father, Son and Spirit, in other words, of his being which is pure love; having already shown that the destiny of humanity is to be and to live in the image of God, we shall define the vital function of God the Creator here as the manner in which the Father reveals his love for humanity as a true principle of creativity.

He reveals it through his creative power; a word that produces life; an action that triumphs over chaos, by placing it at the end of the world; a plan of happiness for a free and responsible humanity.

Creative love makes his creation live as the place where humanity itself constitutes a creative force; a word of love continuously creating a world of love; a permanent struggle against chaos, disorder and destruction; a force capable of transforming the sphere of life into a sphere of happiness.

To call God Father and Creator, is also to affirm, as in good traditional theology, that the human being is human to the extent that he or she shares in the creative spirit of God. As word, he is called to live in a community of creators in which the very exchange of the creative speech among them constitutes a world of love. As masters over chaos, they are the builders of harmony for the advent of a permanent order for the promotion of life. As happy beings they are creators of happiness.

The vital function of the Son, the Redeemer

The Son is the revealer of God's redeeming love for humanity. In him the distant God cut off from the world, becomes closer to us again; he dwells again in a visible manner among us. He lifts humanity out of the fall and leads it into the new communion with the Creator. In fact, he recreates humanity in the breath of God and reasserts God's reign as the true place of life. He re-establishes God's plan for humanity as the only plan of life.

By re-establishing the bridge between humanity and God, by inscribing God's purpose once more in the concrete fabric of human reality, by founding a dynamic of salvation which makes human beings once again capable of resembling the 'Father, the Son and the Holy Spirit' as love, the Son gives to the idea of redemption, a clear and precise meaning:

- the nullification of human destiny as failure, doomed to the determinism of evil and to the fatality of sin;

- the delimitation of essential points of reference to enable humanity to get involved once again in God's purpose, which is both that of the reversal of values through the beatitudes, the fight against all negative forces which destroy human beings and society, as well as the central position of the poor, of the smallest and the excluded, as the very presence of God in the world;

- the opening of the eschatological vision of the new heaven and the new earth as the radical principle which should be the basis for judging human reality.

Once we understand that in the founding myth of Christ's destiny, the Son's role is that of redeeming love, then we can also understand that it is the duty of humanity to constitute itself as reality in the power of this redemption. Human beings are themselves to become redemptive, so to speak, by showing their resemblance to God through the need for every person to be his brother's or sister's redeemer, within a humanity based on solidarity, and called upon to connect its energy of life to the radical eschatological vision of God.

The vital function of the energising Spirit

The Spirit is the guarantee and the permanent force behind what the Son reveals, by firmly rooting God again into the fabric of the world. As breath, force, power and energy, constantly releasing what God proposed to humanity as a way of fulfilment, the Paraclete has the role of transforming the divine plan into concrete action, clear commitments, institutional and social order.

In the Spirit of God, the human world regains its creative and redemptive capacity in order to manifest it in its daily life. We are here in the area of social transformation, where the truth only exists incarnated in facts and concretised in plans for the promotion of life.

The order of the Spirit is a rationally organised fight against everything that undermines human life, a jointly co-ordinated struggle against every principle of dehumanisation and destruction. Whoever gets involved in this order becomes a person committed to struggle and engagement, committed to concrete plans for the building of a new society; a spirit-being, born again in God's reality, who henceforth will not only be its witness but also its breath.

It is clear that the vital function of the energising Spirit defines humanity's very being, or rather what we should be in God. Like the Father's creative function and the Son's redeeming function, the Spirit is an essential element of the Christian vision of the world, proposed to humanity as a way of salvation.

We can easily imagine Africa's total acceptance of, and enthusiasm for, this plan of God, Father, Son and Spirit, and of their order of the mythological founding of human destiny. We can hear clearly the convincing words of the masters of the 'grove of initiation' when faced with Christ revealed in his divine roots and essential purpose.

Welcomed as the revelation of God the Creator, Redeemer and Energiser of humankind, Jesus of Nazareth would thus be understood as the way of the great wisdom of life and the incarnation of God himself in the grove of African wisdom. 'Your God and the god of our ancestors is the same and unique God', as the masters of African initiation would tell him. 'You are his Son, we are his messengers. Let us build Africa's future together.'

This is what we would say of Christ in more modern language: 'The structure of being which you reveal from God, you reveal to us as the very structure of the purpose of our God, and as the web of obligations we must assume in order to build a new society. You reveal to us not only a way of being, but especially a fundamental way of being that is the basis of what it means to be human. It is this that we must promote '

The myth of the calling of a few as the beacon of humanity

In the mythological foundations out of which Christ's character emerges in the African 'grove of initiation', there is the myth of the calling of a small group of people to become the beacon of humanity. As narrated in the Bible in the form of an unquestionable historical truth and an obvious human-divine significance, the myth is presented as follows:

God called Abraham, a man from the city of Ur, and asked him to leave his people and his country, and go to the country to which he would guide him. Abraham left his country and travelled far, trusting in God's promise.

This man, whose entire being was taken up with God's promise, is the 'father' of a family whom the vicissitudes of history brought to live in Africa, in the land of the Pharaohs, in Egypt. Abraham's family lived for a long time on that land, multiplied, prospered and asserted itself by its intelligence and vitality.

When the country fell into a serious social, political and economic crisis, Abraham's people became the object of inhuman oppression, shameless exploitation, and radical and systematic dehumanisation.

God called a man, Moses, from among that race and entrusted him with the task of leading his people out of Egypt. After a long struggle against Pharaoh, Moses led the descendants of Abraham out of Egypt. For forty years they wandered in the desert, moving towards Canaan, the promised land, which God had set aside for them as 'the land flowing with milk and honey'.

After these trials and sacrifices, during which they received the law as the 'Fundamental Charter of the Human', they conquered the promised land after fierce battles, with the help of God and the exceptional intelligence of their generals.

They transformed this country into a beautiful land, had great kings like David and his son, Solomon, after which they fell into disobedience and forgot God. This brought upon them spiritual, moral and political catastrophe. They consequently became divided, were defeated by their enemies and sent into exile in Babylon.

In Babylon, they went through hard times once again, with many humiliations and frustrations. It was a time for a new learning of faith in God and of the internalisation of the demands of his law as a way of salvation. Through the firm determination of the builders of a new destiny, who undertook to rebuild the destroyed temple and restore the creative power of the people, the exile ended and the people went back to their homeland, settled down and lived in the expectation of a Messiah who would restore them to their former state of glory.

When that Messiah came in the person of Jesus Christ, the people did not recognise him, because he did not fulfil the political and apocalyptic expectations of the people of his era. Instead of being a strong nationalist, he extended Abraham's hope to all of humankind. Instead of being a political agitator, he announced God's Kingdom as a radical conversion of being and of society. Instead of being a character whose brilliance imposes God's victory over all evil forces, he was like a seed of humanity in the heart of the world, the starting point of a slow and fruitful process, opening into the future of God.

It is this very Messiah who comes into 'the grove of initiation' for a live dialogue with Africa in search of salvation.

This second myth brings us to essential realities from which the problem of salvation emerges according to Christian perspective: realities we must understand as anthropological and theological bases for the missionary activity of the transformation of humanity and the world.

First of all, there is the reality of promise which does not merely concern the word spoken by God to Abraham, nor only the prospect God offered his people that they should go to the land flowing with 'milk and honey'; deep down it is a basic anthropological fact - the affirmation of the human being and of society as an essential promise to fulfil, a plan to implement.

For we are not beings cast in iron, forged once and for all in a natural or ethnic identity turned in on itself and built on an ancient base which nothing can upset or attack. As in the case of Abraham, the promise is the sign that the human being is in a process of constant enrichment, a process of opening up to major cultures and civilisations where God gradually unveils his will to make us correspond to his eschatological principle, his desire to transform each of us into a blessing for the whole of humankind, that is, a blessing for each man and woman who enters into the arena of our being and our action.

As in the case of the people of Israel, the promise, under the leadership of God, is the conquest of the land flowing with 'milk and honey'. This land is the very land of our being, in the measure that this conquers itself in accordance with God's plan, with God's law shown as the very charter of humankind.

However, there are two hostile principles in the heart of that being, against which we must fight: the Egyptian principle and the Babylonian principle. These include both the human arrogance that establishes oppression, domination, exploitation and dehumanisation as practices of social organisation (Egypt), and the idolisation of human power before which people should prostrate, or rather prostitute, themselves (Babylon).[1]

According to the myth, reality is a constant struggle against the principles of Egypt and Babylon in the name of the principle of Canaan, which is the true symbol of all God's promises to humanity. These promises will be fulfilled inexorably, as his Excellency, Félix Tchotche Mel puts it. What is at stake in this struggle, is the humanisation of the person and society, the establishment of an order of being, according to which politics, economics, social life, moral commitments and spiritual requirements are based on God's Law.

In this way, the wilderness and the exile in Babylon constitute the path to knowledge, the trial through which we understand a fundamental basis for the human, namely, that of sacrifice - sacrifice as the total investment of all forces of being, so as to fulfil God's promise; sacrifice as the force of resistance against the shutting out of the Spirit's breath, and as the power to renounce everything that promotes the forces of social decay; sacrifice as a commitment to put God's cause before all personal causes and interests. In short, sacrifice as the incarnation, in our very being, of the logic of the gift which Christ gave in his destiny as Messiah.

If realities like promise, law, trial, and sacrifice are elements of a fundamental anthropological structure of the myth of the small group of people chosen to be the light of humankind, then it is clear that the emergence of Christ in the African 'grove of initiation' is a process of the universalisation of the Christian faith as a global way of salvation.

This is how we understand it, so as to imagine what the meeting of Christ and the masters of our 'grove of initiation' means: the visionary institution of a spiritual synthesis offered by Christian Africa as a plan for humankind today, the very plan for the globalisation of love and humanity, which we have already mentioned.

In order to carry through such a synthesis, the African 'grove of initiation' does not present itself merely as a place where Christ is welcomed and where his incarnation takes place. It is a creative force which finds in the spirit of the foundational myths of the Christian faith, a ferment that questions the whole history of Christianity as the meaning of existence.

Africa questions Christ on the hegemonic detours which have resulted in closed dogmatic, canonical and theological positions, as well as in a 'discursive policy' which determines the framework and principles of the truth within an established Christian religion that regulates the hermeneutics of the word. Is the worm of this detour to be found in the fruit of the fundamental myths of the Christian faith, or is it a question of falsification by human beings only?

We Africans are all the more qualified to ask Christ himself this question, as we have been both the cultural source of Christian values, and the historical victims of Christianity as the established religion of a western world, handed over to the demons of conquest. Having been to the very sources of monotheism and the religions of the book emerging from the spirit of ancient Egypt, we have lost the capacity for a proper hermeneutics of the meaning of the Scriptures from the time when Christianity came back to our lands as a foreign religion.

From an intellectual point of view, we have been condemned to the awful theoretical practice which the young Dutch theologian, Jan Kranz, calls second-rate theology,[2] that is, the re-introduction into our theology of old concepts and worn-out theories from the West. Again, in order to broaden the issue highlighted by J. Kranz, we can say that we, African Christians, have transformed our churches into places of second-rate Christian teaching, second-rate pastoral care and second-rate spirituality.

In these churches where second-rate theology is preached, we are subjected to the dogmatics and hermeneutics of others, without asking ourselves how those who brought them to us integrated Jesus Christ into the ethico-mythical centres of their world. Is there any connivance between Christ and the religious theories which give themselves ultimacy and which remain forever unassailable in the history of the West?

More profoundly still, how does the structure of being which Jesus of Nazareth reveals as the structure of humanity, and which we ourselves as Africans recognise as a way of salvation, enrich a world where the forces of chaos, the powers of death and destruction still seem to be very active and successful? Can we say that ethico-mythical centres of Christian faith, as we saw in biblical myths, can really be embodied in Africa here and now? At what price, and on what condition, could this be done, and for what purpose?

One imagines here the depth of Christ's silence on these questions and his sudden decision to speak and vigorously assert:

- the non-totalitarian nature of the Word of God as a revelation of the theology and anthropology of creative, redeeming and life-giving love;

- the rejection of any second-rate interpretation of the divine message and Christian faith in their incarnation at the heart of history;

- the right of all peoples to an inventive hermeneutics, whose only standard is God himself in his eschatological project of a new heaven and a new earth;

- the acknowledgement of the original founding myths of African culture as the true path of humankind, a path of anthropological authenticity on which Christ has chosen to march towards God's future in Africa;

- the African continent as 'the new fatherland of Jesus Christ', the new land from where a new plan for the humanisation of the world should take off. This plan is not a theological theory whose principles of rational structuring must be shown; it is rather a concretely lived experience of the spirit of the original founding myths of African society, in the dialogue of life which Africa, even today, has perceived with Jesus Christ, in the light of existential myths which underlie its existence.

The myth of the Saviour tempted by Satan in the wilderness

There is an extraordinary narrative of truth and human profundity in the gospels. Although it is a historical fact recounted by the disciples of Jesus Christ, it has the character of a basic mythological reality, in the full sense of the term. In other words, it reveals what it really means to be a human being. The very elements of the human according to God's plan are laid out with impressive realism.

In order to continue to show Christ in what he brings as the essence of life in the 'grove of initiation' and in the main problems facing the African continent, we thought it useful to take this narrative from the gospel as a christological yardstick for understanding salvation. The narrative is as follows:

> Jesus returned from the Jordan full of the Holy Spirit and was led by the Spirit into the desert, where he was tempted by the devil for forty days. In all that time he ate nothing, so that he was hungry when it was over. The devil then said to him, 'If you are God's Son, order this stone to turn into bread'. But in reply, Jesus answered 'The Scripture say,s "Man shall not live by bread alone"'. Then the devil took Jesus up and showed him in a second all the kingdoms of the world. 'I will give you all this power and all this

wealth', the devil told him. 'It has all been handed over to me, and
I can give it to whom I choose. All this will be yours, if you
worship me.' Jesus answered 'The Scripture says, "You shall
worship the Lord your God and serve him only". Then the devil
took him to Jerusalem and set him on the highest point of the
temple, and said to him, 'If you are God's Son, throw yourself
down from here. For the scripture says, "God will order his angels
to take charge of you". It also says, "They will hold you up with
their hands lest you dash your feet against the stones". But Jesus
answered, 'The Scripture says, "Do not put the Lord your God to
the test".' When the devil finished tempting Jesus in every way, he
left him for a while (Lk. 4:1-13).

Resounding in the heart of the 'grove of initiation', this narrative
poses the problem of the identity of Jesus as a manifestation of the
true man according to God's plan. The entire strategy of the devil is to
compel Jesus to get into what could be called the battle of true human
identity: to manifest himself as what he is, not according to God's
plan, but according to the idea given to him by the tempter, or more
precisely, according to what the populace expects of the Messiah as
the revelation of the true man in his relation with God.

In the general conception that people have of him and the issues
which the devil as the revealing figure defines here, the God-man or
more exactly the man transformed by the spirit of God, must be determined by three main realities.

The first is the central position of the "belly" as a radical principle
of his desire. In the name of the belly, there could be a reversal of
values in which God and the Absolute are placed at his service by
using magical and miraculous means, by opening up to hidden and
dark forces which reject God. The devil invites Jesus to submit to the
despotism of the belly and thereby put humankind into subjection.

Christ rejects this identification of the human person. He shows it
for what it really is, namely, escape into a false existence. The authentic God-man, the true human being, is not identified by anything
other than the higher values to which God calls humanity. The belly
should be subservient to these values and not the other way round.
But what are these values?

The second temptation clearly defines them. In the eyes of the
devil, the God-man should be identified by the accumulation of
wealth and material things which impress others, and base his life on
the principle of material assets, and define himself in relation to an
external principle of alienation to property and appearances. But
Christ shows that such a principle of alienation reduces humanity to a
false existence, in other words, to pathetic despotism, futility and triv-

iality. It is on this superficial register that the devil plays, himself the epitome of falsehood, to reduce people to a false existence and subject them to the domination of the powerful. Once we embrace a world view based on acquisition and share its values, we are compelled to submit to the law of inequalities which society itself raises to the level of an ontology of essential distinctions determined by wealth. This is the world of domination, this is the jungle where economic and political 'cannibalism' tie their millstone to the neck of the whole society. In such a society, the weak and the poor represent all that is negative. They are nothing because they do not have anything. They are worthless because they have neither material wealth nor power.

Christ rejects such a world and sets in opposition to it, God's plan, the central values of which are those of the service of God. And since God becomes incarnate in the smallest and most neglected neighbour, it is in serving this poor and wretched neighbour that authentic humanity is measured, that is, the divine force operating in humanity. It is not simply the question of being sensitive to the poor, but of liberating them from their poverty by changing the social structures of injustice and inequality, as the liberation theologians of Latin America have understood so well.

To help the masters of the 'grove of initiation' better understand the significance of human authenticity, Jesus will have recourse to two other stories which, to us, are an integral part of the myth we are analysing here: the story of the good Samaritan (Lk. 10:25-41) and the story of the last judgement (Matt. 25:31-46).

Human authenticity is truly revealed only when the man attacked by thieves and left to die finds, on the road to his death, the way to life which another man opens for him. The good Samaritan is authentic, not only because he helps his brother, but because he goes all the way to physically and socially rehabilitate his neighbour's integrity. He is authentic because he brought back to life the Jew who had been attacked by thieves, by giving him possibilities of new life. It is this new life which is the true goal of the values of service which Jesus proposes.

According to Jesus, this is the ultimate reckoning, on which we shall be judged as human beings in the light of the revelation of God's humanity. By identifying himself with the hungry, the thirsty, the destitute and the prisoner who need other people to restore them to true humanity, God clearly shows where the central principle of authentic life lies. This principle is not external to the person or society, but is a radical internal principle because it shapes our sensitivity to what is negative in others, as E. Dussel says in his book, *Community Ethics.*

Against the principle of alienation, Christ therefore establishes the internal sense of service as the measure of human values. All values deriving from this sense of service are values of true humanness, such as solidarity, sharing, mutual support and joint commitment to shared happiness. It is God's will that we in this world, live, love, learn or change in the direction of these values. This is the real world of God, the authentic world of humankind.

The third temptation concerns the centre of the system of action for the transformation of reality. According to the devil, the epitome of inauthenticity, the action of changing reality should be similar to what is already required by the first temptation: a performance of magic, carried out from a completely magical conception of things, where, by using occultic formulae, wonders were achieved without effort or serious investment of oneself. All that is required is an 'abracadabra' for one to defying all the physical laws created by God and throw oneself from a tower.

Jesus also shows at this level that the central principle of human action is not in a magical and spectacular mystifying hoax, but in the responsibility assumed in accordance with God's purpose. It does not lie in the use of extraordinary psychic power to change the world, but in the ability to harness the 'ordinary' forces that God has given to human beings to use to build the world. It is not with miracles that we change the world, but with the quiet strength of the human spirit which the Lord has filled with his kindness. So it is pointless tempting God, testing him to act in our place. He has already done what he had to do. It is up to us now to do what we have to do.

It is to be understood that throughout this commentary, reference is being made to Africa and to the necessity of changing her systems of desire, knowledge and action.

From the depth of the 'grove of initiation' where we welcomed him, Christ shows us that it is neither by the centrality of the belly, nor by our alienation, nor by faith in esoterism and occultism, that we can overcome our crisis. The way of salvation is human authenticity according to God's purpose, which is the inner depth of the human being.

Faced with such a requirement, the masters of the 'grove of initiation' can only say of Jesus: 'This man is truly the Son of God'.

Footnotes

1 For these principles, we have drawn once again from the thought of Enrique Dussel, the theologian from Latin America, whose book, *L'éthique communautaire* (Paris: Cerf, 1991) (English: *Community Ethics*) is a great source of information and reflection, and is very helpful in understanding salvation in Jesus Christ

today. We are also indebted to José Comblin for his book, *Anthropologie chrétienne* (Paris: Cerf, 1991), from which we derived useful comments on the vision of the human being and society according to God's Spirit.

2 After a stay in Latin America and after teaching theology in Cameroon, Jan Kranz became convinced that the weakness of African theologians lies in their inability to innovate theological hermeneutics from African realities. Old concepts from the West which they consider as inherent to theological thought cannot lead them to a profound embodiment of their theologies in African peoples and in basic Christian communities. Even if he does not take into account all the on-going struggle to assert an inventive and credible African theology, the remark is appropriate. It deserves serious consideration for the future orientation of theology in Africa.

CHAPTER 10

Problems and their christological relevance

A problem of creativity and resourcefulness

Following the use we have just made of the ethico-mythical centres of African culture and of the founding myths of the Christian faith, we are already hearing objections from right-thinking people and those who cast doubt on the creative force of African vital energy.

'Oh', they exclaim, 'there they go again with their old negro tales, worn-out chatter and fuss about African authenticity and personality, coming out of their tombs to serve as a reminder to the new African generation. Should we not warn the youth against all these outmoded theories and place before them only the challenges that really matter today, namely, the scientific, demographic, military, economic and political stakes on which the quality of life and future prosperity depend? Why still talk about tales, myths and legends of the past, when Disneyland, the world of 'Dallas' and 'Dynasty', and the entire fiction of Hollywood are becoming world-wide in a new global and incurably materialistic spirit? When will black people stop dreaming about the purity of the 'exquisite corpse' of their negritude or blackness, so as to fully take control of their present and future destiny in the world?'

All these questions have for a long time agitated our minds. They have filled our books and the whole course of our reflection since the end of 1975, when we set ourselves to write philosophical texts.[1] While relying on modernity as a framework for the development of Africa and for the improvement of its quality of life, we sought, from year to year, for new ways of evangelising Africans who had become very 'modern' and very 'future-oriented', and who have broken with the ghosts of old decrepit ancestors and the host of forefathers defeated by the storms of history.

It was at the end of the research that we carried out in African churches at the beginning of the 1990s, that we realised that we were wrong about the people we were evangelising. The very modern and very future-oriented African, who fascinated us as students and young researchers, was merely a convenient illusion, a silent figment of the imagination.

During an evening we spent together at an international symposium organised by the Institut Théologique et Missiologique Eugène de Mazenod, in Kinshasa (Democratic Republic of Congo), in February 1994, the theologian, Oscar Bimwenyi-Kweshi, warned us against confusing the core values of a culture with events of the recent or distant past which punctuate its historical evolution. Like his fellow countryman, V. Y. Mudimbe, he recalled that the past is not behind us but in us. He recounted many current cultural facts which show that the African world view is made up of fundamental realities which shape the relationship between Africans and Jesus Christ. He assured us that nothing essential or important has been lost or destroyed. 'The grove has not been burnt.'

In our analysis of the problem, we had always thought that this grove was a place and that its values could be defined. Philosophically speaking, we were looking for the structure of beings in terms of depths of being and the mystery of existence. We wanted to define entities only from the perspective of structuring energy and the plan of destiny - conditions that would make possible the assertion of being as being, of culture as culture, society as society and of the African as an African.

During the discussion with Bimwenyi-Kweshi, we understood that what he referred to as the 'grove of initiation' was to be interpreted more in the light of the word 'initiation' than the word 'grove'. To be more exact, it was to be interpreted in the light of the relation and the semantic clash between the two words. In this way, it was not a place to inhabit once more, but power to initiate again, to relaunch and to re-envision: a creative breath which makes the initiated a different man, a new being, born again in the spirit of his own culture, his vital force.

When we began, in the SCAT Academy and in the project of the Academy of African Thought, to undertake serious research into the meaning of the 'grove of initiation', it became clear to us that we were dealing here with something important for the mastery of the present and the creation of the future.

Many of us decided to delve into the area of secret societies and the African world of initiation, to become full members of our own world in Africa, and thus discover the vital laws which give the initiated an ontological force that is superior to that of the uninitiated person.

For our own part, we became personally interested in the problem of the relationship between the African power of initiation in the full and comprehensive sense of the term, and Christianity as dynamic of initiation. We soon realised that what is important in the African 'grove' is not the control over the mysteries of the invisible or the learning of magical or mystico-religious formulae. Rather, it is a way for each person to become really human, the way to relationship with the creative breath which gives the human being the possibility to discover and create the most effective solutions in the fight against the forces of death, evil, despair and darkness.

This relationship is the essential thing and not the rites which surround it. These rites are merely visible catalysts or symbols of the transformation of being, and of the need for good to triumph over evil.

If the creative spirit is what matters, then one can understand why those who did not bother to look into themselves and into their own world to establish vital links with the human element at the basis of their being, are insignificant, inconsistent and debased in their existence.

Thus the problem of identity stopped being a problem of theological theorisation and became an anthropological, social and missionary one.

An anthropological problem: How do we form creative personalities, persons capable of dominating the vital space where they blossom and so receive a really human face?

A social problem: By what means does a society become creative and affirm itself as a dynamic force for ethical invention.

A missionary problem: What type of evangelisation should be undertaken to create innovative societies and personalities?

These issues of creativity and resourcefulness are important for the Africa of today. In the life of African church leaders, as in the activity of pastoral agents and leaders of Christian groups and movements, these problems constitute a real test for the mind. Often taking the form of a question as to whether one can be a Christian and an African, this issue is, in fact, that of the invention of a vital synthesis where a new kind of Christian should be born, creator of himself and of his destiny: the Christian-African (the hyphen here means that it is not an issue of the relationship between a noun and an attribute which qualifies it, but two words which now form one body and one spirit, from the depths of the Christian faith).

The theology of African ethico-mythical origins and the very mythical bases of the Christian faith as we have outlined them, is not an answer to this problem. It only defines possible conditions leading to it. Should we master these conditions, we shall be able to release the creative dynamics in us, and the resourcefulness which exists in our societies, so as to become really African-Christians (the hyphen still means the mark of a strong semantic and anthropological unity, but this time, from Africa itself in its core values).

Basically, what is most important is not the result we obtain nor the cultural wealth we reap by entering the 'grove of initiation', but the very movement by which we decide that there is in one's very being and in one's own culture, the basis for releasing creative forces.

There is no doubt whatsoever that these forces should be strengthened as much as possible by the ethico-mythical centres of the Christian faith as Christ would present it to the masters of the 'grove'.

Should the meeting of Christ and these masters not, therefore, be considered as the real way to salvation for Africa? It should, if our ambition is really to think of the future and 'to invent a new image of ourselves'.

Christian faith and the problem of organisation

In our research on basic problems on which evangelisation should focus in contemporary African society, we were struck by the recurrence of problems concerning the sense of organisation which is lacking in our people and in our countries.

Daniel Kilem Mbila, the Cameroonian economist, first pointed out this problem in his role as organiser of development projects in Central African churches, through a non-governmental organisation (NGO) he was running in Brazzaville at the time we met.

In the numerous conversations and discussions we had together during the sessions and symposia which both of us led, or in which we participated as resource persons, he kept returning to this problem with obsessive energy. Analysing critically the failure of many African public institutions and structures, and extending this to include nation states, he showed that the lack of the spirit and principles of good organisation is the root cause of most of our problems. Being more of an economist than a philosopher, more pragmatic than theoretical, he had set in motion an extensive programme of action in churches for the development of Central Africa. This involved the training of a new type of pastor: organisers of their pastoral activity and architects of projects according to organisational ethics based on the gospel and the logic of the talents.

D. Kilem Mbila was fighting against the type of spirit which his fellow countrymen, Daniel Etounga Manguellé and Axelle Kabou, would later reject with their concepts of 'cultural adjustment' and of the 'refusal to develop', respectively. He was criticising a certain aspect of African culture as a culture of passiveness, parasitism and vagueness.

In our work as pastors, we were struck by the pertinence of Daniel

Kilem Mbila's analysis and the link he made between the problem of organisation and the logic of the talents in the gospel.

Through his work, we realised that to evangelise is to organise people and teach them to organise themselves so as to prepare for the advent of a society worthy of God's plan. It means attracting men and women to work for global social change based on a principle of organisation peculiar to the gospel, that is, the vision Jesus had of talents and their management, which is that of the effectiveness of a rational, rigorous, as well as ethically-oriented administration of the talents that God entrusts to us.

The perception of this very problem articulated by His Excellency, Félix Tchotche Mel, must be noted here. Right from the first contacts we had at the beginning of the 1990s, he spoke to me at length of the Harrist Church and of how it derived all its strength from the management, administration and mobilisation of human resources, that derived from the deep sense of dignity of Africa, as well as from the respect which Afro-Christian churches should have for themselves in the world today. A social psychologist by training, he did not look at the problem of organisation from an economic perspective, but rather from that of the human desire to rely on oneself and be responsible for one's own destiny. Contrary to many African churches which are mainly dependant on external funding, the Harrist Church relies solely on intelligence, determination, vision and solidarity. 'It is human capital which is the basis of social happiness', Felix Tchotche Mel continues to assert, and rightly so. Combining action with words, he launched a major programme for the training of the leading lights in his church in order to boost creativity and organisation. His pastoral activity made us sensitive to the human dimension of organisation, and to the truth of the principle which states that, in order to walk, you must stand on your own feet and begin to take the first steps.

The third person whose approach to organisation impressed us very much is the Congolese politician, A. Mbuyi Kalala, Chairman of the *Rassemblement pour une nouvelle société* (RNS), a movement for civic and political action to change life in Africa. In his approach to problems which is in keeping with his scientific training and his project of political effectiveness, he refused to play the game of most politicians by dishing out money to buy consciences, to ensure popularity or influence the electorate. Rather, following a purely educational approach, he travels to African towns and rural areas and speaks on a one-to-one basis with those who are likely to be involved in social change, without bothering them with verbose and harmful ideologies.

Slowly, patiently, without any waste of energy, or loss of time, and with a strong disposition, a calm, placid nature which commands respect, and the ability to convince and ensure the support of others, he views organisation as a prerequisite for the social, political, economic and cultural revolution of the continent. 'Everything is done step by step'. He kept saying as he went from place to place, that when determined and motivated men and women are committed to restructure their being for a new society, we shall undoubtedly win the battle for the future.

Having become committed to the process of the African member churches of the Evangelical Community for Evangelical Action (CEVAA) to revive and renew theological activity and missionary commitment, Mr Mbuyi Kalala helped with the African co-ordination of this project, to bring to light that the gospel and organisation go hand in hand, and that Jesus in Africa should be presented not only as a teacher, a healer and a servant of people, but also as an exceptional organiser who has been active down the ages to transform the mind and to revolutionise the consciousness. That is the gospel of change.

For our part, we know that in the present situation of our continent, there is a problem of a theology of organisation which calls for a new Christian education and a new understanding of the gospel, according to both the logic of productivity shown by the parable of the talents, and to the principle of a rational and forward looking vision Jesus Christ talks about, when he urges people to read the signs of the times and not venture into projects without first weighing all the consequences.[2]

Many theologians are also convinced about it today. They are engaged in reflection which considers this problem, analyses it clearly and incorporates it in a christology of salvation for the Africa of today.

Christology of salvation and the problem of vision

In the ecclesiastical vocabulary of contemporary Africa, the word 'vision', comes again and again as a leitmotiv which every church leader and every Christian, however uneducated, likes to use, at the risk of overuse.

Since the international meeting organised on the theme, 'Where there is no vision, people perish', by the Federation of the Union of Christian Students Associations (FUACE) in Brazil at the beginning of the 1990s, the All Africa Conference of Churches (AACC) has made the word 'vision' so widespread and popular, that it has become a major requirement in many churches. In Côte d'Ivoire as in Cameroon, in the Democratic Republic of Congo as in Rwanda, in Benin as in Equatorial Guinea, there is talk not only of programmes to implement and projects to draw up, but especially of a vision of the future to promote.

The problem is that the exaggerated use of the word 'vision' often conceals serious disillusionment with the actual prospect that African societies have of the future, and the way in which African churches project themselves into the future.

Apart from Jubilee 2000, which has mobilised Christians in some countries, as well as the numerous missionary symposia where professional theologians and church leaders meet, the vision of the gospel in African society beyond the year 2000 has not led to major investigative research, nor to widespread popular support in communities, parishes and grassroots movements.

What shall churches look like in the next century and throughout the next millennium? What society do we want, as African Christians called upon to build a new Africa? What long-term direction are we giving to our mission? What major changes shall we make to African existence in the years to come?

If these questions come up now and again, then the time has come to no longer consider them as merely rhetorical, but to include them in the African dynamics of the quest for salvation.

In the first part of our reflection, problems of the insignificance of our being, the inconsistency of our action and the devaluation of ourselves in our own eyes and the eyes of others, have conditioned our manner of viewing the problem of salvation and its relationship with our systems of desire, knowledge and action. In the same way, the conclusion to our reflections will centre on problems of human creativity, social organisation and the prospective vision of ourselves in relation to the new society.

Footnotes

[1] As a matter of fact, it was in December 1975 that the review *Zaïre-Afrique* published our research, thus making us known as philosophers and theologians. At that time, problems relating to development and liberation were prominent in African thought. A quarter of a century later, the same problems are still current but the theoretical framework has moved on. We have taken note of it and are re-examining once more the basic problems relating to the destiny of our continent.

[2] The issue of talents consists in multiplying what we have received from God. He who has received ten talents should produce twenty, he who has received five should produce ten, etc. The talents referred to here are not only economic and financial, but also the general management of human resources and social realities. As for the logic of a rationality that calculates and anticipates, this is what

Jesus demonstrates in his parable concerning a general who goes to war and expects to be always informed about the number of soldiers on the other side, so as to decide whether to fight or negotiate. Like this general, everybody should examine the significance of events and act cautiously and in an enlightened manner. It is the gospel of fruitfulness and effectiveness in action.

CHAPTER 11

African theology and the building of a new society

How has African theology perceived Jesus Christ and his act of salvation with regard to the problems of creativity, organisation and vision, which we consider here as the possible condition for social transformation and the building of a new society?

Two phenomena draw the attention of any observer of the current African theological scene:

- the increasingly visible reconciliation between theoretical and academic christologies, on the one hand, and popular christologies on the problem of salvation in Jesus Christ, on the other;

- the emergence of new theologies which seek to base the new African society on the vision of global humanism as a project for the globalisation of the human, today and in the future.

Narrowing the gap, reconciliation of theologies

For a long time, Africa has given the impression of being a continent divided against itself so far as theology is concerned. On one side, there were the theoretical and scientific researches in which those who studied these subjects have failed to get to grips with their own findings:

- missionary theologies of the *tabula rasa*, the founding or planting of the Church, through which relationships between Africa and the Christian faith were conceived within the framework either of a demeaning interpretation, or as part of a quest for the fulfilment of African aspirations in Christian religion, or the introduction once again of dogmatic truths, liturgical practices and discipline already developed in the Western Church;

- the theologies of adaptation, indigenisation or inculturation, a vast theoretical field where missionary theologies were challenged by the firm desire to develop an African Christianity, designed, conceived and experienced by Africans themselves through their creative intellect and concrete hopes;

- the theologies of liberation which laid the foundations for Africa to tackle the major economic and socio-political challenges of today, in order to build a future marked by dignity, freedom and prosperity;

- theologies of reconstruction which advocated the end of colonialism and neo-colonialism, and the advent of a free post-colonial African thought, devoid of all the problems of pessimism and defeatism, oriented towards the construction of a free and democratic society, nurtured by the big dreams of returning to historic initiative, and propelled by a vigorous energy of responsibility and resourcefulness.

Alongside these rationally constructed academic trends, there existed countless strong theological and religious emotions, whose fervent word touched the spiritual depths of the people:

- theological and missionary practices of great African prophets whose strategy consisted in reviving 'the early moments' of Jesus Christ in the Africa of today through miracles, healings, cleansing, deliverance and the preaching of a powerful gospel, capable of defeating the forces of evil;

- charismatic and pentecostal mysticism that came from popular American-type Christianity where what dominates is the logic of witnessing, persuasion, fascination and the dynamics of praise;

- the 'frenzied' preaching of sects and new religious movements described by an African theologian as 'the unpaid bills of established churches'; that is, these sects and religious movements spread where the churches had abandoned the everyday challenges of illness and health, deadly occult forces and the divine strength of life, deliverance from demons, and the quest for peaceful brotherly communities.

Whereas only a decade ago, these two types of theologies were opposed to each other, they have been made to reconcile by the very evolution of African society.

The sudden entry of the people of God into the socio-political field has led to a growing interest among theologians and ecclesiastical authorities in the real cries from suffering African people, in particular, the cries from the masses for healing and deliverance, calls for release from spells, and for exorcism, the fight against supernatural forces and the powers of evil unleashed by the demonic in society.

It is important to note that exorcism, which was a domain somehow reserved for sects and marginal churches, has now forcefully entered the established churches. The amount of suffering caused by demonic forces has led the masses to look up to the priests and pastors for powerful delivery of the Word of God and powerful acts in this area. Not only are we gradually rediscovering Jesus as healer,[1] but we are beginning to understand, as theologians, that the practices of deliverance and purification constitute an integral part of preaching and of missionary action.

This has led theologians such as Monsignor Milingo of Zambia, Father Hebga of Cameroon and Father Abekan of Côte d'Ivoire,[2] to theorise about the struggle against the devil.

Since their research responds to a real problem in society about which the Church cannot remain silent, such research has ceased to cause amusement or arouse misunderstanding and irritation. A new theology of illness and evil is thus emerging. This new theology gets to grips with popular visions of human suffering and the answer God offers in Jesus Christ. The new theology thus theorises about a practice which professional theologians and religious authorities are discovering anew, without it giving rise to any serious conflict between recognised university research and the hermeneutical wealth of the African people of God in everyday life.

Just like the sudden entry of the people of God into the socio-economic and political field, and the interest of theologians in the suffering of people caused by sorcery, witchcraft and witch beliefs, there is another trend emerging which is reconciling theological reflection with Christian social practice at the grassroots. This is marked by the spirituality of enthusiasm, emotional exaltation and warm, mystical power, where Christian communities are rejecting cold, calculating and dominating reason, in order to feel God in the very depths of the passion of the African person.

This spirituality is aggressive, conquering and irresistible, and constitutes a veritable tornado of missionary activity which used to irritate professional theologians not very long ago, and now requires that they pay close attention to its meaning in an African society faced with socio-economic and political problems and the terrible powers of sorcery, witchcraft and witch beliefs.

The interest of theology in this spirituality, in its extraordinary successes and the threats it poses for the future, is of extreme importance. It brings one to understand that such a massive phenomenon does not occur by chance. It calls for an in-depth analysis, for an understanding of its beneficent effects so that its dynamics may be harnessed to make it fruitful for our society.

Instead of demonising its effects, or dismissing it as cultural imperialism which has found in Africa a favourable emotional and metaphysical terrain, it is better to see in this spirituality, the emergence of elements of a new theological and spiritual framework, a framework that gets established churches involved in a work of discernment, acceptance, restructuring and reorientation, as has happened in Catholic communities in several countries through some of institutionally well-organised charismatic and pentecostal movements.

As a matter of fact, Africa has a duty to give to this movement a fruitful and comprehensible understanding of the problem of salvation in Jesus Christ. It is the duty of theologians and church leaders to get down to this task. Many are already doing so and are thus bringing their theological knowledge of African destiny closer to popular quests for salvation in Jesus Christ.

Long standing theological issues and new dynamics of salvation

In this new context, the long standing issues dominating African theology are acquiring a new meaning. Their vigour and public drive regarding cultural identity, inculturation, liberation and reconstruction are now mobilising minds with more lucidity and discernment than at the time of the militant agitation of the 1960s to the 1980s or at the time of agitation for democracy at the beginning of the 1990s. Distinct from ideological passions and sterile quarrels of the past, these questions are shaping a new theological awareness directed towards the new century and millennium, and are of a different order from those that theologians have used as the force of theoretical reflection and form of socio-political commitment for about forty years.

What is the difference between these theological positions as they are currently being articulated and the spirit that dominated the African theological field not so long ago?

Until now, the articulation of issues was essentially combative. The theologies of identity were opposed to the theologies of European missionaries of the beginning of the century. Liberation theologians denounced research on identity. It all developed according to a dialectic of theoretical and scientific confrontation, where the people of God were more the objects than the subjects of the discourse.

By keeping the matter at the level of discussions between specialists and by not initiating a process through which theological ideas would deeply motivate the people of God, we were confronted with a distressing situation of a perpetuation of empty ideas that did not produce concrete plans for social transformation. Except in the area of inculturation where debate led to major liturgical reforms, African theology found no incarnation in public life. It was not easy to say who actually represented it. For apart from some professional theologians, no social movement assumed responsibility as the historical force for the embodiment of theological ideas.

While all our theologies set themselves the task of changing our destiny, they were not perceived by the people of God as theologies of salvation. Salvation concerned only the beyond, the last judgement, heaven or hell.

It is only now, with the emergence of popular theologies of healing, deliverance and exorcism, that people have started to perceive the relationship between all these problems and the general state of society, as if society itself was suffering from a vast pathology of possession, with political, economic and social crises as the consequences.

In the light of the recognition of the demonic as a common phenomenon, the people of God are beginning to understand that we live in societies 'possessed' by evil forces, and are now in search of comprehensive exorcism comprising all the forms of our theologies.

The spirituality of enthusiasm and exalted feeling becomes in itself the place of salvation not only for the individual, but also for society as a whole, with its quest for identity, liberation and reconstruction.

In our opinion, the theological writings of Monsignor Milingo, Father Hebga and Father Abekan on the fight against the demonic in African society, are the first works to expose the problem of salvation in such a way as to fill the gap between academic theologies and people's expectations. They also present the problem of salvation in such a way that African ancestral traditions regarding illness and health have a decisive place in the theology of healing in Jesus Christ and in current scientific research on the role of psychic powers in individual and collective stability.

We consider these theological writings not only as a new source of dialogue between African tradition and modernity, but as real bridge-theologies between the different trends in spiritual research on our continent. In other words, they are forces of cohesion based on a practice whose language the people understand and whose power they experience with as much vigour as theoreticians analyse their meaning.

Being themselves the first reflections which the masses, overwhelmed by suffering, understand, these writings constitute the basis for a comprehensive understanding, the main dimensions of which should be reflected upon again from this basis.

Similarly, the spiritualities of struggle against the demonic which evangelistic and pentecostal movements are spreading everywhere in Africa, are the theological bases which can serve as a point of departure for reflection on salvation in Jesus Christ from a global perspective.

It is useful to consider these spiritualities, as well as the theologies of exorcism, as a basis for thinking about the future of salvation in Jesus Christ, in Africa.

Exorcism and evangelical charismatic spirituality as bridge-theologies

In the practices of exorcism and evangelical charismatic spirituality, there is no word that is used or exalted more than the word 'salvation'.

'Are you saved, my brother?' 'Are you saved, my sister?' Such are the questions around which revolves the whole process of healing, deliverance, exorcism and resounding victory over demons and the forces of evil.

What exactly does salvation consist of? What does it represent when perceived from the perspective of the meaning of existence, opened up by the message of Jesus Christ?

A closer look at the research of Monsignor Milingo, Father Hebga and Father Abekan, who devoted their ministry to the struggle against the devil and the forces of evil, shows that what is at stake in salvation is mainly a world view where reality is a network of forces. This is both a biblical and African understanding by which we know that certain forces can live in some people, places or social structures, in order to spread evil. Forces that destroy human beings, forces that 'destabilise' individuals and forces of decay in societies, are the terrible realities which bring disease and death. They are responsible for physical and psychological disorders whose symptoms are easily detected by specialists.

In the Bible, Jesus brings salvation through healing where these forces are driven away from the persons they haunt and the spirits they abuse. Salvation in the Bible has a physical and psychic dimension which consists of deliverance and purification whose effects are seen by all.

But Jesus goes further in his understanding of healing. According to Professor Francis Grob, our colleague and specialist in New Testament studies, of the Ndoungué Protestant Higher Institute of Theology (Cameroon), Jesus is aware of the fact that physical and psychic evil is closely related to political and social evil. When the demon Jesus was driving out revealed his name by saying, 'I am Legion', one must have been totally deaf or obtuse not to have understood that the term by which he called himself was neither politically nor socially neutral. It was leading listeners directly to the Roman 'legions' that terrorised citizens and created martyrs in Palestine.

In reality, Jesus was saying clearly to his disciples and to the crowd that the physical and psychic disorders from which many people were suffering, were partly linked to the total system of state control and human administration. The demon, the evil spirit and Satan were socio-political forces which took possession of people so as to disturb their minds and destroy their vital power and energies. The target of these forces was humanity itself and what it means to be human. This had to be destroyed in society, in people's minds, consciences and hearts. It had to be destroyed in social relations and in community life.

The goal of the theology of exorcism and deliverance is to re-establish the person and society in what is truly human. That is what Jesus accomplishes. That is salvation in Jesus Christ.

When we examine African society, we realise that the realities spoken about in the Bible are not light worlds away from our present realities. They do not refer to mystical and mythological visions of reality which a post-Christian modernity can neither understand nor endorse. These realities describe massive phenomena and experiences which Christians and churches of Africa are facing. In their current African manifestation, they take the form of sorcery, witchcraft and witch beliefs.

These are demonic strongholds par excellence; principles by which evil operates and possession occurs. It is a question of appropriation and manipulation by the forces of evil in order to destroy people, disorganise society and spread death.

Witchcraft is the dynamic by which these forces inhabit a person, possess him and drive him irresistibly to 'eat' others, destabilise them and destroy them. Whatever forms this operation takes: mystical and supernatural (a grandfather mystically 'eats' his grandson who then dies) or socio-economic and political (the Head of State 'eats' the budget of his country and thus ruins the nation), the basic reasoning is the same; whether it is the spirit of a person or that of a society, it is cannibalism as desire, as spirit and as a way of being.

But what is important for its effectiveness is the belief society has in witchcraft as a system, the totality of beliefs, canons of interpretation of reality and the mental structures which constitute the popular imagination. It is the effect of the total system and the collective imagination upon the individual, that constitutes the demonic.

The conclusion to be drawn is that the theology of exorcism is, on the one hand, the fight against distress, helplessness and suffering of which individuals are victims, and, on the other, the fight against the socio-economic and political mechanisms of the demonic.

Today the problem of salvation in Jesus Christ cannot be presented without serious reflection on the strategies of individual deliverance and the techniques of fighting against the damaging effects of the evil system on the entire society.

In practice, the fight against the demonic at the individual level is carried out with weapons which satisfy the people. The ministry of Monsignor Milingo in Zambia, that of Father Hebga in Cameroon as well as that of Father Abekan in Côte d'Ivoire, reveal all its tools: prayers of deliverance, laying on of hands, pacification sessions and head-on attacks upon the forces of evil, among others. With sure successes and with failures of which exorcists themselves are fully aware, this ministry gives a concrete idea of salvation, of what can legitimately be expected from faith in Jesus Christ in the African society of today: the complete re-establishment of the individual in his physical, moral and spiritual being, that is, in all his natural creative forces.

It is doubtful whether at the level of demonic activity as a socio-economic and political system, reflection on salvation and deliverance has as yet produced convincing results. It is also doubtful whether the analysis was conducted with theoretical tools that enable Africa to present to the world a collective and common theology of salvation, based on the re-appropriation of the memory of our history and the power of our popular vision. Considering the world as a network of forces or as a hierarchy of powers in a structure of confrontation, collision, conflict and antagonism, does not explain how one may fight in the name of Jesus Christ against the social structures of sin, or against the demonic experienced as an entire order of life.

It is here that a bridge should be established between the popular expectations of deliverance and exorcism, on the one hand, and the theoretical analyses of the theologians of liberation or reconstruction, on the other.

Basically, these theologies can be presented to the people of God as mechanisms by which the devil is driven away from the community and the society as a whole, with the prospect of enabling these communities and societies recover their basic stability, physical and spiritual health, morale and creative ability.

The same thing can be said of the domain of sorcery as a system of thought and action in society. It is noteworthy that the fight against witchcraft in Africa is carried on more by visiting traditional healers than by confidence in the work of evangelism carried out by the churches. The reason for this is basically a general outlook which believes that the solution to problems is to be found in the realm of invisible forces in which human beings are merely puppets. In fact, it is the exaltation and generalisation of theodicy: this belief in the all-powerful nature of a supernatural and occult providence which can protect people and societies without involving their responsibility and freedom and even less their initiative and creativity.

All the activity of Jesus Christ is directed towards the fight against these witch beliefs and their concept of theodicy that minimises human responsibility. Even where Christ advocates absolute trust in God, he does so before men and women re-established in their being by the Spirit, conscious of their historical capacity for action and destined for the practice of responsible solidarity, which is at the heart of the divine project for humankind.

Pledging allegiance to, and adopting witch beliefs, has seriously weakened Christianity in Africa. Confusion has often arisen easily between trust in God and submission to the power of witchcraft. As F.

Eboussi Boulaga, the philosopher, strongly asserts, the spirit of witch-craft has settled not only in the popular Christian imagination, but also in the conceptual canons and theoretical protocols which established mission and evangelisation in Africa from the dawn of modern times.[3]

There was a time when the justification for the evangelising project was based on the perceptions of salvation assured by a divinity much closer to life insurance in the beyond or here on earth, than to the God of Jesus Christ, in his plan to establish people and societies and to restore them to their being and make them agents of their own history. For a long time, there has been a considerable struggle against traditional religious cults and not against witch beliefs. Witch beliefs, as a type of spiritual outlook, has even increased as traditional religious cult objects were transformed either into objects of art for tourists or into rearguard cultural forces for Africans in quest of identity.

It is the drift of this Christianity, that today requires the setting up of a common front for reflection and action between, on the one hand, the struggle of evangelical and pentecostal spirituality against trust in false gods, and on the other, the struggle of the theologies of liberation and reconstruction against the spirit of witch beliefs in the heart of Christianity and in the socio-political field.

This reconciliation is gradually taking place through the rediscovery of the message of indigenous African prophets like Simon Kimbangu (Democratic Republic of Congo, Central Africa and Congo-Brazzaville) and William Wade Harris in West Africa (Côte d'Ivoire, Ghana, Liberia).[4]

In these prophets, we find a concept of salvation in Jesus Christ which is far from any spirit of witchcraft, a spiritual message rooted in the socio-economic issues of the recovery and the affirmation of the creative freedom of individuals and people, as well as those of the struggle for the independence of African countries and the building of societies based on dignity, prosperity and holistic development.

When we re-appropriate for ourselves the image of Christ as found in the indigenous African Christian prophets at the height of the colonial period, and interpret it in the light of the current struggles of the evangelical and charismatic movements, and of the liberation and reconstruction theologies in Africa in their fight against the witch beliefs at the heart of a theodicy that reduces and destroys human responsibility, there is the feeling that a new era is beginning, an era of of anti-witchcraft ecumenism which promotes an outlook freed from witchcraft and witch beliefs, and works for the advent of a liberated society. This ecumenism fights against the demonic not only in the spiritual and religious field where the principles of submission and abandonment to a discouraging hereafter operate, but also in the socio-political domain. The Africa of today has become conscious of the stakes of such an ecumenism even if reactionary denominational forces are still trying to pull it back towards rearguard antagonisms. In the small marginal group most determined to build a new society, it is not doubted that the future belongs to this vitally committed ecumenism, which is responsible for the promotion of the human.

The same can also be said of the fight against the spirit of magic, against this type of naive and blind faith in recipes for miraculous success, empty slogans and mystifying 'abracadabras' which produce irrational attitudes, by playing on words and manipulating hollow symbols, thus pretending to act on reality at the very point where this reality proves resistant to the incantations of false prophets and the tellers of perpetual good fortune.

There was a time when the African Christian faith, in its presentation of sacraments, devotion, dogma and profound mysteries of Christianity, gave the impression of being a religion cut off from the quest of human intelligence for understanding. For each important question on the Trinity, the two natures of Christ, resurrection, the virgin birth of Jesus Christ, or the real presence of the Lord in the eucharist, those undergoing Christian instruction, children and adults alike, were given the answer, 'It is a mystery'. The debate was thus closed and the process of making the minds of people childish became irreversible.

Even today, it is outrageous that many Christians with weighty and serious responsibilities in their society still hold onto their childhood catechism without seeking to reflect on the Bible and the Christian faith with the understanding and mature mind of an adult. In their mind, Christ remains the reality of a magic formula; and his salvation, the reward of a magician.

This falsification of Christianity took its toll on the Christian perception of responsibility and the Christian spirit of being responsible for oneself in order to change reality. Today, things are gradually changing and attitudes are being transformed, perhaps because the social conscience itself is caught up in the movement of the quests and achievements which have to do increasingly with the sense of responsibility, liberation and creativity. The Christianity which is emerging and asserting itself in Africa is increasingly shaped by the struggle against the spirit of magic .

In this sense, all the major trends of African theology since independence were theologies of struggle. They have never supported the popular transformation of Christianity into a magical religion. Whether theologies of identity, inculturation, liberation or reconstruction, all of them are united in the desire to build a society where the struggle for basic freedoms, human rights, democracy, development and human dignity, is based on religious conscience backed by the need for Africans to assume their status as beings created in the image of God, that is, as essentially and profoundly creative beings.

Footnotes

[1] We refer here to the excellent reflections of Father Cécé Kolié: 'Jésus guéris-seur?' in *Chemins de la christologie africaine*, 167-92. See English text in R. Schreiter (ed.), *Faces of Jesus in Africa*.

[2] Cf. Gerrie ter Haar, *L'Afrique et le monde des esprits, le ministère de guérison de Mgr Milingo, Archevêque de Zambie* (Paris: Karthala, 1996); Meinrad Hebga, *L'Afrique de la raison, Afrique de la foi* (Paris: Karthala, 1996). Less directed towards a philo-sophical or theological theorising, Father Abekan's account of his struggle against the devil is an eloquent testimony to the nature of the popular outlook and beliefs.

[3] Cf. Eboussi Boulaga, *Christianisme sans fétiche* (Paris: Présence Africaine, 1981).

[4] At the beginning of the last century, these two prophets launched two spiritual and socio-political movements based on the ability of Africans to be responsible for their destiny, to change the relations based on domination that they had faced during the colonial period, in order to make the Bible and the Christian faith theirs for the purpose of a project of social transformation which is still current at the beginning of the 21st century. It is in this global project that the fight against witchcraft became an essential element of the action of Afro-Christian churches. Simon Kimbangu led this fight in Central Africa, in present-day Democratic Republic of Congo, where his followers have built today a Kimbanguist Church which is very active in missionary work. William Wade Harris led his crusade of conversion and evangelisation in West Africa, especially in Côte d'Ivoire and Ghana, where his followers belong today to a Harrist Church conscious of its spiritual wealth and have decided to participate vigorously in the building of a new African society.

CHAPTER 12

Envisioning the creation of a new African society

It is our view that the phenomenon of the reconciliation between academic theologies and popular practical theologies, and the new situation where theologies of the Catholic, Protestant and evangelical charismatic churches find themselves engaged in the same activity, constitute the manifestation of a new and yet common way in which Christian Africa is tackling today the social problem of creativity, organisation and the vision of a new society.

We are just coming out of a distressing period where churches had developed their pastoral strategies without anchoring them in the challenge to transform minds according to a clear vision of the future, a concern to promote the creative spirit and a strong determination to harness the living forces of our countries towards a new destiny.

The need to tackle this problem is becoming increasingly obvious in theological discussions which make salvation in Jesus Christ a basic issue, not only from a biblical and eschatological perspective,[1] but also from the perspective of the total transformation of hearts and minds for the building of a new society.

We can say that today the vision is beginning to take shape, it is beginning to offer salvation in Jesus Christ as a major contribution to the cultural renewal, political renaissance, economic reconstruction, moral regeneration and the spiritual renewal of Africa.

Salvation here refers to the construction of an African society reconciled with its history, restored in its capacity to take initiative in history, and motivated by the strong determination to produce a reformed humanism, in which politics and economics would once more be enriched by humanitarian ethics incarnated by Africa and Christ in their meeting in the heart of the symbolic and cultural resource of our 'grove of initiation', this place that makes possible a new creativity for African Christian faith.

The vision of this humanism leads to the promotion of African cultural and spiritual creativity, and to the working out of practical ecumenical and inter-religious syntheses. Here, all the active forces come together to mobilise and develop concrete projects, where human life may be nurtured though the fertile soil of the African 'grove of initiation' and the powerful forces of the gospel, which Africans welcome in the truth of their being and in the openness of their spiritual journey to all the potentialities of their identity.

What Africa gives to the world in the domain of creativity, is the wealth of this open identity, its ability to blend in itself great treasures received from its 'multifaceted, scattered and multiracial identity open to the world, sure of itself, and we could add, joyful', according to Achille Mbembe.[2] It is in the creativity peculiar to this self-conscious identity, that African Christianity would offer to the world lessons of a peaceful plurality, of a serene ecumenism and of a fertile inter-religious dialogue. It is in this creativity that Africa would display its majestic liturgical inventions, its warm relationship with God and its communal ethics, capable of launching Christian communities into all the decisive battles for the future. It is in this creativity that churches, through the gospel, could drastically renew politics, the economy, society, culture and life in Africa.

There would be at the heart of Africa, a concept of salvation that is essentially creative of the relationship with transcendence. African persons saved in Jesus Christ would be truly creative, seeing in the gospel the true directions for the use of powers of resourcefulness, that make them human.

Presenting a hermeneutics of resourcefulness as a fertile ground for the reading of the Bible today, is giving hope once more to Africa and opening doors of hope for the building of a new society.

But the resourcefulness referred to here is not only an individual phenomenon. It is a communal venture where creative men and women decide together to change the society and mobilise their resources and their power to build the future, from a strict sense of organisation of mission and evangelisation based on the plan of Jesus Christ, Saviour and Redeemer of humankind.

In order to promote this hermeneutics which opens the way for a creative and inventive spirit in the light of the gospel, a real ministry of hope is necessary: a work that requires closeness to others, and interpersonal or public education, centred on concrete projects for human advancement and the humanisation of society. Christians together would implement these projects based on their readiness and ability to organise themselves, in order to change the destiny of our continent, as is now the case in several African non-governmental organisations, or in some parishes which have decided to serve as places of hope.[3]

Today, all African theologies can be read as ways to this requirement of a ministry of hope. This constitutes the essential principle of their intelligibility as a contribution to the problem of salvation in African society.

Even if these African theologies are still confronted by opposing forces which want to perpetuate a Christianity of other-worldly salvation, with hopes directed towards heavenly divine realms in their intoxicating brightness, it can be said that they require a radical horizon for this ministry. Their goal must be the creation of a visionary, creative and resourceful society for the struggle against all the negative forces that Africa is suffering from, the debilitating powers of sorcery, witchcraft and witch beliefs, and the socio-political and economic powers, that are embodied in harmful and sterile institutions and social structures, whether local or international.

It is in the struggle against these negative forces that the idea of organisation takes on a truly theological dimension: in the perception of the personality of Christ as the heart of the project for society, the building of a social order organised spiritually in creative solidarity and liberating love; organised not like the world, but in the light of the purpose of God, that is, the salvation of humankind.

In other words, insofar as the plan of God is the salvation of the world, the pastoral task required today is that of organising the people of God and Christian communities for new activities and new strategies for social change, and for building a new society. This is indeed the task of a new evangelisation of Africa in this new millennium.[4] This means organising the people of God to prepare themselves effectively to face the major problems of destiny and the problems that plague us everyday.

African churches, where they are most alive and most enlightened, already understand the importance and the urgency of this issue. There was no religious authority, no church 'leader' among those we met during our research, who was unaware of the requirements of the mission of evangelism as the ministry of hope for Africa, as a matter of urgency for the building of an Africa of hope.

In the theological world, there is the same awareness where already there is a strong determination to establish theological ideas firmly in the movements for socio-economic and political change, which the spiritual and moral power of the gospel would permanently enrich.

In this atmosphere, churches are gradually helped to appreciate better the enormous human and material wealth which they have, and to really open up to each other for the same ministry of hope and the building of a new African society.

That, precisely, is the great vision which spurs on the most enlightened of their members. They are coming gradually to understand that the great religious dynamics which came from elsewhere cannot continue to work in a disparate, conflicting and antagonistic manner, according to a spirit of hegemony and power which have nothing to do with Jesus Christ.

They also understand that wherever the ministry of hope is exercised (in temples, chapels, houses, streets, markets, companies and state institutions), and in all social sectors which should incarnate it (movements, occupations, associations, non-governmental organisations, grassroots communities, prayer groups, networks of civic and political action, ecclesiastical authorities and any person of good will), evangelism as the dynamic for the building of the new society requires a real and profound meeting, without any complacency, between Christians and all sectors of society. This would not be with the attitude of converting them to 'the true religion', namely, Christianity alone, but in the spirit of enriching them with the new humanism which the personality of Jesus Christ, welcomed into the 'grove of initiation', sows in people's consciousness and imagination.

It is necessary to single out as a consequence of this idea, the gathering of churches themselves at the heart of the profound realities of Africa, of our ancient symbolic and spiritual resources out of which they should be radically re-created, 'born again', according to the energising Spirit of Christ, now incarnate in our 'grove', the African Christ, 'our brother who has become God and God who has become our brother', 'our son who has become love and love which has become our son'. If we consider the future of African Christianity in the light of this requirement for each religious community to meet others in the heart of the 'grove of initiation', it is obvious that dogmatic wars and parochial quarrels which divide them will appear as what they are, namely, inessential battles and often pathetic and futile conflicts where nothing of the 'essential of the essential' of the Christian faith mentioned by Father Varillon, is involved. They will receive from the heart of Africa a new christological norm, born of the dialogue of Christ with the depths of Africa where we and our history meet as the home, as Oscar Bimwenyi-Kweshi has already revealed, of our creative force and our understanding of the human.

The role of the 'grove of initiation' where Christ has taken his seat is better understood here. It is not a place of folklore nor an essentially religious stronghold where Africa would make fun of itself in the game of its own mythical identity vis-à-vis the West; nor is it an exotic commodity which African theologians would put on the current religious market in order to be seen and to boost their standing as creators of concepts. It is even less a hackneyed 'nigger' tale brought out to rehabilitate the ancestors or a mystifying social voodooism with nothing essential to contribute to the present world. Rather, it is mainly an issue of the emergence of a new norm for African christology, where the salvation of the continent is considered from a perspective of a creative humanism and global ethics.

'Creative humanism' does not mean a philosophy that places humanity at the centre of the world as the sum total of everything, 'man as the final and supreme value', according to the expression of Jean-Paul Sartre, but it means the process whereby human destiny is found in the discovery of the bonds of life which unite humankind to the whole of creation and to all the spiritual forces which constitute reality, bonds which also unite the past, the present and the future in the building of one and the same vital awareness by which, here and now, we are responsible for our past and our future.

Basically, in creative humanism, the main reality is, as we saw in our analysis of myths, the desire for relationship, the care we must take to honour the human energy we inherited, to enrich its creative dimension in our present, and to think about the future in terms of the need to enrich humanity by bequeathing to our children a world in which people can really live a better life, a world in which God, humankind, the invisible and the visible, that is, the whole of creation, can be honoured in the deep bond which unites them in the heart of our consciousness of life.

In such a perspective, we become human only in proportion to the care we take of the relationship, through the vitality of the concern to promote the ethics of the relationship, that is, the human as the meeting ground of the powers of reality to be assumed in the meaning of life, here and everywhere.

In the 'grove', a vital relationship has developed between Christ and Africa. We can no longer consider life as if this relationship never existed, as if the fate of our destiny as creators of the world, and the destiny of humankind as a whole had not depended on this relationship. We cannot live as if we had not perceived, in the Messiah of Nazareth, a higher level of humanity below which our ethical and spiritual conscience would no longer allow us to live. We cannot conduct ourselves as if, in this dead and resurrected Christ, nothing of ourselves is revealed to recognise the gospel as the true way of humankind. We Africans who are witnessing the beginning of a new millennium with many anxieties and great hope, are ourselves carriers of a powerful energy of rebirth, of renaissance, re-creation, reconstruction, regeneration and renewal, namely, Christ himself as the heart of a new creativity in the vitality of our being, in all the spiritual, symbolic and material resource, which today should be used for building a new society.

If the relationship with Christ is henceforth so important to us, it can only be the source and the foundation for other relationships in life which we can establish with the whole world, the whole of creation.

This is why this relationship with Christ leads inexorably to a universal ethics that African Christianity can help in creating, from its concern for relationships, the quality of the links we establish between peoples, countries, cultures and civilisations; the quality also of the links that join us to the forces of the plural historical memory of humanity and the dreams of a better world by which we want to build the future of humanity as a future based on solidarity.

If Christ is perceived, in the spirit which he extends to the heart of the world, as the very substance of the ethics of our relationship, it is not only African life which will be completely transformed, but also humanity as a whole in its political, economic, social, moral and spiritual relationship.

A new society would be born: a new society nurtured by the dream of the globalisation of humanity and of love, a new society enriched by the desire for a new heaven and a new earth. It is the society of salvation in Jesus Christ, the main goal of the mission and evangelisation of Africa on the outset of the third millennium.

Footnotes

[1] This perspective was analysed in a decisive and convincing manner by Father Paulin Poucouta in his book, *Lettres aux églises d'Afrique, Apocalypse 1-3* (Paris: Karthala, 1997). In this profound and serious book he uses all his biblical, exegetical and hermeneutical understanding to illuminate the major issues at stake in the Church's mission in the light of all the problems of salvation in contemporary African society.

[2] A. Mbembe, interview in the Magazine, *L'Autre Afrique*.

[3] The shining example we have here is that of the Catholic parish of Tokombéré in Northern Cameroon, a great place for human advancement where the phrase, total development', has concrete power which changes the society.

[4] We shall soon publish through Karthala Publishing House, Paris, a book devoted to this problem of the new evangelisation. In it we develop more amply those points presented here in a rapid and synthesised manner.

CHAPTER 13

Conclusion

Africa as theatre for the globalisation of love and humanness

In order to carry through this meditation on the issue of salvation in Jesus Christ in contemporary African society, we decided to take as a guide, three groups of issues which seemed important to us in thinking about the future of our continent.

First, we considered issues relating to the insignificance, inconsistency and devaluation of our being in the world today.

We then examined the problem of the dictatorship of 'the belly', despotism, alienation and the tyranny of the powerlessness we endure in our current daily life.

Finally, we studied problems concerning the need to promote a spirit of creativity and organisation, as well as a global vision of a future which would correspond to our great dreams in life.

In order to respond to these concerns and to consider them from the perspective of salvation in Jesus Christ, we drew from the fundamental values of African culture, the riches of the biblical revelation which illuminate the image of Christ and current research in the African theological field.

It seemed to us that Jesus of Nazareth is to us:

- a spiritual dynamic who is internal to our culture, to our living traditions and to the original founding myths of our existence from time immemorial;

- a radical and critical otherness who reveals to us our strengths and weaknesses, and also reveals to us the heart of God: the being who is totally love, and whose destiny is to call human beings to be transformed in his love;

- a challenging exteriority, that is, a historical figure who came to our land through the cultural canons of the West, which, henceforth, forms part of our spiritual itinerary.

Christ thus understood, leads us to consider the issue of salvation as the problem of the very meaning of life in Africa:

- meaning as the re-appropriation of our creative spirit through a spiritual alternative operating in the meeting between Jesus Christ and the wisdom in our 'grove of initiation';

- meaning as the desire to build here and now, the new African society, to take in hand the tasks of cultural renewal, economic reconstruction, political recreation, moral regeneration, and spiritual renewal which is incumbent upon us;

- meaning as open-mindedness to God's radical plan for the world: the prospect of the new heaven and the new earth.

In Christ, this dynamic of meaning has enabled us to give definite shape to the project of civilisation which Africa should offer as the way of salvation to humanity in quest of a future: the globalisation of the human, and of love, a true theatre for the manifestation of humanity's resemblance to God.

Works by Kä Mana

Méditations (poem) (Bruxelles: Editions de l'Archipel, 1985).

L'ontologie musicale de mon plus bel arbre chanteur (poem) (Bruxelles: Editions de l'Archipel, 1986).

Une poétique philosophique: de l'anthropologie et l'imaginaire à l'esthétique évocative (Louvain-La-Neuve: Nouvelles Rationalités Africaines, 1986).

L'homme, la question éthique et l'idéologie économique, réflexion (Bruxelles: Editions de l'Archipel, 1986).

L'expérience poétique de la transcendance: Dieu, l'être et le sens et la poésie française contemporaine (Kinshasa-Libreville-Munich: Publications Universitaires Africaines, 1987).

Destinée négro-africaine, expérience de la dérive et énergétique du sens (Bruxelles: Editions de l'Archipel, 1987).

L'Afrique va-t-elle mourir? Essai d'éthique politique (Paris: Cerf, 1991. Second edition, Paris: Karthala, 1991).

Théologie africaine pour temps de crise, christianisme et reconstruction de l'Afrique (Paris: Karthala, 1993).

Christ d'Afrique, enjeux éthiques de la foi africaine en Jésus-Christ (Paris-Yaoundé-Lomé-Nairobi: Karthala-Clé-Haho-CETA, 1994).

L'église africaine et la théologie de la reconstruction, réflexions sur les nouveaux appels de la mission en Afrique (Geneva: Centre Protestant d'Etudes, 1994).

'Pour l'éthique de la vie: Bible, écologie et reconstruction de l'Afrique', in *Ethique écologique et reconstruction de l'Afrique* (Yaoundé-Bafoussam: Clé-CIPCRE, 1997).

Pour le christianisme de la vie et pour l'Afrique de l'espoir (Paris: Karthala, 1999).